# Retreat

# of the

# Soul

*Reflections on the Contemplative Life
by the Bardstown Brothers*

*Editors:*
Gregory H. Sergent
James M. Wells

# Retreat of the Soul

Scripture references are from the:
King James Bible for Today (KJBT)
King James Version (KJV)
New International Version (NIV)
New King James Version (NKJV)
New Living Translation (NLT)
New Revised Standard Version (NRSV)

To order additional copies of this book contact:
James M. Wells
P.O. Box 216
Norton, VA 24293

jmwncc@icloud.com
ghsergent@yahoo.com
hopewaybooks@gmail.com
amazon.com

Cover Photo
Crabtree Photography
Wise, Virginia

Other photos used by permission

HopeWay Publishers
Gate City, Virginia 24251
HopeWayBooks.com

# What others are saying...

I've just finished *Retreat of the Soul* and I'm tempted read it again right now. I'll do so soon, and repeatedly. The writing is as uncluttered as the subject, the premise is intriguing, and the ideas are consistently uplifting. There's a small spiritual retreat on every page, and I savored the marvelous mingling of traditions described in the chapters. In a loud age, how we need some hushed and holy hours! In matters of the soul, strategic retreat is necessary for spiritual progress.

Robert J. Morgan, Author, Pastor, Speaker

This is a most refreshing compilation of writings from a gaggle of "Free Churchers" telling their journey into contemplative spirituality. They boldly go where few "Free Churchers" dare go, yet they maintain the integrity of their distinctive denominational practices and worship styles. Allow them to take you on their pilgrimage into the contemplative spiritual discipline where they find deeper pools of thirst-quenching waters that not only refresh their souls but give more strength for their personal ministries. Follow them into the deeper life and relationship with God that can only come with silence and solitude."

Tim Sturgill, Chaplain, USAF (Ret)

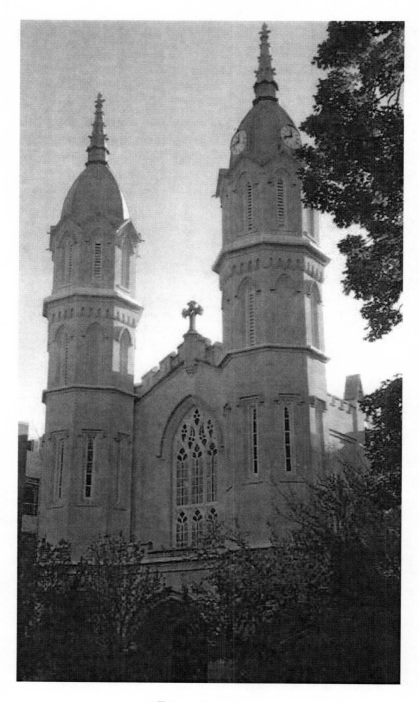

*St. Vincent's*

Nazareth, Kentucky

I feel honored for the privilege of reading *Retreat of the Soul*. The very first thought I had as I read it was: "You know what? I really need this!" I truly believe that my own spiritual life will be enhanced by reading this devotional piece. How marvelous that ministers from different theological traditions and backgrounds are willing to ask, "What can we learn by observing the spiritual disciplines of Trappist monks?" In a time so terribly superficial, especially in spiritual matters, it is thrilling to read about the Bardstown Brothers and their desire to know God in a more intimate way! This is my prayer: "Lord, use these men and their devotional book to deepen the prayer lives of believers. Amen."

Dr. David Enyart, Retired Professor
Johnson University

Retreat of the Soul may be the only book that I have ever read from front to back in one sitting. As a public official, I rarely have the time. I must confess that often I am too distracted with "life" to concentrate for more than a few short moments. In today's fast-paced, busy, and inter-connected world, distractions are every-where! We rush from one task to the next with a furious speed. Yet, as this collection of writings reminds us, we all need to slow down, disconnect from the world, seek a place of quiet worship, and reconnect with God daily. I hope that you will be as challenged, encouraged, and strengthened as I was reading every page.

C.H. "Chuck" Slemp III, Commonwealth's Attorney
for Wise County & the City of Norton, Virginia

*Abbey of Gethsemani*

Trappist, Kentucky

✠

*THESE REFLECTIONS ARE*

In honor of

*Dr. Jerry Mattingly*
Bardstown Retreat Founder

And dedicated to

*Dick "Skip" McGuirk*
An original "Bardstown Brother"

*SPECIAL THANKS*

To the *Sisters of Charity* of Nazareth, Kentucky
who graciously host the annual
Bardstown Brothers Retreat

To the *monks and staff* at Abbey of Gethsemani

To *Cheryl Redman* for her consulting expertise
and labor in proofreading

To *Dr. David Enyart*, retired professor of Bible, homiletics,
and pastoral ministry at
Johnson University for selfless
mentoring and invaluable suggestions

✠

*O God, you are my God; early will I seek you: my soul thirsts for you, my flesh longs for you in a dry and thirsty land, where no water is;*

*To see your power and your glory, so as I have seen you in the sanctuary.*

*Because your lovingkindness is better than life, my lips shall praise you.*

*Thus will I bless you while I live: I will lift up my hands in your name.*

*My soul shall be satisfied as with marrow and fatness; and my mouth shall praise you with joyful lips:*

*When I remember you upon my bed, and meditate on you in the night watches.*

*Because you have been my help, therefore in the shadow of your wings I will rejoice.*

*My soul follows hard after you: your right hand upholds me.*

*Psalm 63:1-8 (KJBT)*

# Table of Contents

✠

# Forward

✠

In the spring of 1982, five Johnson University Ministry students, led by one professor, traveled from Knoxville, Tennessee, to "Our Lady of Gethsemani" Trappist Monastery in Trappist, Kentucky, for a three-day retreat. They were challenged to observe the vows of silence and prayer for those three days. That experience had a deep impact on those students and it has led to a lifelong tradition of returning to Gethsemani for an annual retreat that we now call "A Retreat of the Soul." Our group has expanded and changed over the years, but the purpose is always the same: to experience fellowship with brothers in ministry and learn from our experience in a religious culture very different from our own.

We are very grateful that professor (and our friend), Dr. Gerald Mattingly, exposed us to something wonderful that we would have never done on our own. Either fear of the unknown or ignorance based on preconceived ideas told us that we had nothing to gain from such an experience. We are in debt to Dr. Mattingly (Jerry) for pioneering a spiritual experience that has had lifelong consequences for all of us.

Jerry is from Louisville and his father grew up near Trappist, Kentucky. Because of that, Jerry spent a great deal of time around that monastery and heard many stories from his father about his childhood in the shadow of Gethsemani. His experience led him to challenge us to take that first retreat and the rest is, well, "history."

*So why are we writing this book?* After many years of retreating, praying, worshiping and sharing fellowship together at Gethsemani we decided that we wanted to leave something that might have the same impact on others that Jerry had on us. Our lives have been altered in unique and important ways by our spiritual retreats. Writing a book of reflections is our answer to that question. It is our desire to personally share in an informal way how these experiences have impacted our spiritual lives and our pastoral ministries. After reading these testimonies we encourage you to take a retreat of the soul.

Thank you, Jerry, for mentoring us and for sharing with us in in this life-altering experience. Many blessings to all who read these words and grow in their appreciation for the ministry of Trappist monks.

*Jeff Noel*

# Contemplative Prayer

✠

*Chapter 1*

Jeff Noel

Why would a non-denominational pastor of a contemporary style church want to spend time at a Catholic monastery? In fact, why would this be a recurring pattern for 35 years? That is a great question. In fact, the heart of this collection of essays is the answer to that question for each of the contributors to this book of reflections.

For me, it has to do with two driving elements. First, what did Paul mean in 1 Thessalonians 5.17 when he said, "pray continually"? Second, can I learn anything from a Trappist monk about prayer, ministry and my relationship with Jesus? Let me share some of my observations and why I think time spent in retreat at the monastery – alone or with a group of fellow pastors – is one of the most centering experiences of my spiritual formation.

Let me briefly address the first question. My understanding of Paul's teaching to the Thessalonians to "pray continually" is an encouragement to be a contemplative. In other words, *contemplative prayer is a practical expression of Paul's exhortation to 'pray without ceasing.' It is a lifestyle of conscious living in the presence of God and walking in communion with Him in the midst of everyday life.*

This is my attempt to capture the practical essence of living a life of continual prayer -- which in my understanding is being a "contemplative."

I will revisit this biblical conclusion at the end of this essay, but with that in mind let me address the second question -- What can I learn from a Trappist monk? -- in order to lay a foundation for my exegesis of Paul's words.

First, it is important to understand that for Trappist monks, prayer is considered ministry. They do not view prayer as a passive act. To the contrary, I have observed their practice of prayer as a means to connect with the power of heaven to bring God's Kingdom to earth. In fact, many believe that the monastic movement and the institution of Benedictine Rule (the rule of order for a Trappist monk) was actually the vehicle that preserved the church through hundreds of years of corruption and abuse in the Church.

The monks preserved the heart of being Christ-followers through their simple life of prayer, work, study and humility. Their efforts to reach into many parts of the world and establish monasteries in remote parts of Europe and the new frontier of America became the mission that expanded the reach of the gospel all over the globe. So instead of retreating from the world, the monastic movement was literally an advance of the gospel.

This understanding was a total reversal of my preconceived understanding of monks and the monastic life. Spending time at the monastery on retreat and studying their history on my own revealed that prayer for a monk is an effort to saturate the world with the gospel and undergird the ongoing ministry of the gospel by seeking the Lord to empower His work through the church. For a monk, prayer is both a personal pursuit of knowing God (which I will address later) and a ministry of intercession to advance the Gospel to the lost. In truth, a monk views his cloistered life as spiritual warfare engaging the enemy on the frontlines of battle in the spiritual realm (Ephesians 6.10-18).

There is no question that this understanding has had a deep impact on my concept of prayer. Seeking Jesus for His Kingdom to invade the realm of the earth is a powerful and divine act. Prayer is not a "retreat" from God's work but is high-level engagement here on earth. When one views prayer as ministry – as does a monk – then the "work" of prayer becomes essential to God's mission on earth and reaches a level of importance that grows beyond a simple devotional act that pleases God. I no longer underestimate the power of prayer, and that is a lesson I learned from the monastic life that translates into my daily walk and ministry.

Second, for a Trappist monk, the reading and recitation of Scripture is an act of prayer. Every day monks observe the seven divine hours as they step away from other activity and meet in the church to recite Scripture according to a yearly lectionary, through means of chanting and song. The main focus is the Psalms, with attention to the gospels and epistles. In the course of a year monks recite the Psalms and dozens of other Scriptures multiple times. They do this as a means of prayer. Knowing that the "word of the Lord does not return void" they regularly "pray Scripture." I have

5

studied that concept and even taught others the importance of using the words of Scripture as a basis of prayer, but the most powerful example of this for me is the daily life of a monk. What I used to consider a ritualistic liturgy devoid of meaning and power is now a vivid demonstration of trusting in the powerful spoken word of God.

It seems clear that all Christ-followers -- monks or not -- need to have a consistent liturgy of the God's word in their life. This is part of being a contemplative and becomes a powerful memory tool to internalize and digest Scripture. I think this is exactly what David meant in Psalm 119.11: I have hidden your word in my heart that I might not sin against you.

Continual recitation of the word of God helps internalize its truths and guards our hearts from disobedience. It literally embeds the word of God in our hearts and minds. With the words of God emblazoned on our hearts, are we not empowering ourselves to live in His presence? When His words are not far from us, neither is He. His words are the constant conversation of a contemplative life lived in communion with Jesus - a life of prayer. I have learned this from Trappist monks.

This has impacted me personally and it has made a difference in how we worship corporately at the church I serve as pastor. Even in the midst of a very contemporary worship style with a full band, powerful sound system and theatrical lighting, we have rediscovered and incorporated the power of liturgy and the spoken word. It is not a meaningless responsive reading but powerful corporate prayer lifting the Word of God in worship. We have not instituted monastic chanting, but the journey is not over yet!

Lastly, Trappist monks embrace their life of silence as an opportunity to deepen their relationship with Jesus. In truth, this realization has had the greatest influence on me. My first trip to the monastery in 1982 with a group of college classmates was simply to observe and learn about monastic life. It had a deep impact on me.

As we shared in the observance of the "silence vow" and participated in the services, I was profoundly moved by the culture. I certainly had no desire to become a monk-but I did make a decision to become a contemplative in the midst of a busy ministry life. The benefit of silence and contemplation while reading Scripture and growing in my relationship with Jesus hit a new level.

I didn't understand the sincerity of the monks them-selves at first glance, but over the years I began to understand that in a very different way than I pursued Jesus, the monks pursued Him as well. Their sincere pursuit of Jesus and a desire to know Him became obvious. I was struck with the sacrifice they were willing to make in order to pursue Him. Was I willing to pursue Him with the same passion in the midst of pastoral ministry and life in the world? Could I be "in the world but not of the world?"

The reality is that pursuing a contemplative aspect of life has been the thing that teaches me how to do that very thing. Knowing that the presence of Jesus is with me and in me, regardless of the situation that swirls around me, has given me a peace in the midst of storms. I learned this from my observation of monastic life and my experience of retreats at the monastery. These are my "centering experiences" that remind me of the value of silence and contemplation in the middle of a busy ministry.

I am truly grateful for my experiences at Gethsemani and the fellowship enjoyed with brothers in ministry and a tradition that has spanned the centuries. These times are truly a retreat for the soul. With that said, I conclude my observations by revisiting Paul's admonishment to the Thessalonians to "pray continually." In reality, the life of prayer has nothing to do with posture or words or place. It is all about a relationship with Jesus. Praying continually is living with the constant awareness that we are in the Presence of the Spirit of God.

Being a "contemplative" has very little to do with our religious tradition, call to ministry, or our engagement with or withdrawal from the world. Instead it has everything to do with staying before the Lord in our hearts and minds. Living in His presence is literally the act of continual prayer. As Brother Lawrence said in his notes to a novice monk, it is "the practice of the presence of God." To that end, I commit my life to the pursuit of a contemplative lifestyle; in every aspect of my life I seek to "pray continually."

# "Silence Spoken Here"
✠

*Chapter 2*

James M. Wells

*"...and after the earthquake, a fire, but the LORD was not in the fire; and after the fire a sound of sheer silence.  When Elijah heard it, he wrapped his face in his mantle and went out and stood at the entrance of the cave."*
*-I Kings 19.12,13, NRSV*

## The Sisters

Once a year, in the fall of the year, the Bardstown Brothers make a pilgrimage to the beautiful and peaceful campus of the Sisters of Charity Retreat Center in Nazareth, Kentucky, just outside of Bardstown.

And it begins.

We come apart from the world for a few days for prayer, fellowship, study, rest and recreation.  We leave our families, our homes and our ministries and move into the guest house on the grounds of the retreat center, where we become a temporary part of a community of nuns. Yes... nuns!  They welcome us with the love of Jesus and are as amused by us as we are by them.

At one of our retreats we were blessing the cafeteria with rather loud laughter and one of the sisters came over to our table and asked who we were. When we told her, she smiled and replied, "I never would have guessed you were all ministers." We took that as a compliment. There is a quiet dignity and joy about the sisters and the community in which they live that is difficult to put into words. Maybe some things are not meant to be put into words. Maybe that applies to what I am attempting to do here, but I shall continue.

## The Monks

On Friday evening, we journey to the other side of Bardstown to Trappist, Kentucky. There, tucked away the rolling hills, is the Abbey of Gethsemani, the oldest Trappist monastery in America, founded in 1848. The Abbey describes itself as a school of the Lord's service, a training ground for brotherly love. Following Christ under a rule and an abbot, the monks lead lives of prayer, work and sacred reading, steeped in the heart and mystery of the Church. The monks who live, worship and work there are part of the Order of the Cistercians of the Strict Observance (OCSO).

For the 25 or so years I have been part of Bardstown Brothers, our worship with the monks is the most anticipated part of the retreat. As soon as I set foot on the grounds of the monastery I sense an ancient atmosphere. I sense something holy, something attractive, something inviting. I sense . . . the silence. I feel . . . the silence. Silence permeates the place. It is noticeable. It is, as the saying goes, deafening. It is awe-inspiring, but not threatening, not alarming. There is security and serenity in the silence. There is something natural about it. And like an old friend I have not seen in a year, it greets me. And it teases me, as friends often do, by whispering, "Where have you been?" And I enjoy its presence.

## The Language

One of the clever ways of requesting silence is a simple sentence found here and there on the grounds of Gethsemani: "Silence spoken here." It is an appropriate way of saying it.

Three words.
Five syllables.
Seventeen letters.

It would not do to say, "silence observed here." Or "silence practiced here." Or "silence encouraged here." Or "silence needed here." Or "silence demanded here." No! "Silence SPOKEN here." Silence, itself, is a form of communication rarely spoken in our noisy world. In silence we speak to God, and in silence God speaks to us.

God speaks in the silence of the heart.
Listening is the beginning of prayer.
*Mother Teresa*

We need to learn to speak the language of silence. It is very much like learning to speak another language. It takes time, effort, patience and practice. And we learn best by doing.

Silence is a good thing. A practical thing. A spiritual thing. A wise thing. Someone said, "Speak only if you can improve upon the silence." Even those wise words have their basis in the Bible, with its many teachings about controlling the tongue. "Be quick to listen, slow to speak, and slow to get angry" (James 1.19, NLT). "There is a time to be silent and a time to speak" (Ecclesiastes 3.7, NIV). We have traditionally interpreted Solomon's words as knowing when to speak and when not to speak, the Old Testament equivalent of James 1.19. But could he mean more than that? More than simply keeping one's mouth shut in order to refrain from sinful speech, fueling an argument or revealing foolishness?

Yes, there is a time when words are needed, but there is also a time when silence is required in order to hear the wisdom of God, appreciate the greatness of God and enjoy the presence of God. According to the Teacher, there is a time for the language of silence and we must take the time and, if necessary, make the time.

Silence may have been part of the reading, praying, and singing of the Psalms, the contemplative prayer book for God's people. By praying the Word of God we best pray the will of God, and silence can contribute greatly to that end. The term "selah" appears many times in the Psalms; according to scholars one possible meaning of "selah" is "pause." And the logical thing to do when we pause in praying the Psalms is to be silent before the Lord. In that sacred silence we delightfully meditate (Psalm 1.2) on His Word and "nourish our souls with a lofty idea of God" (Brother Lawrence). Silence is an undervalued language. Selah!

### The Inner Monastery

We keep good company when we enter sacred silence. Jesus often retreated to be alone with His Father

(Matthew 14.13; Mark 1.35; Luke 5.16; Luke 6.12, 13; Luke 11.1, 2; John 6.15), hearing only the noises of nature, which undoubtedly contributed to the silence and solitude He desired. This empowered Him to walk resolutely through this world with peace, purpose and perseverance that caused others to be amazed. If He made space for silence, how much more should we?

Solitude is often needed to do this, but not always. Inner silence, the silence of the soul, can be experienced and can prove profitable even in crowded places. One can retreat into one's soul (solitude) while sitting in a packed waiting room or sipping coffee in a busy McDonald's. Joseph Dispenza, in "The Splendid Spiritual Practice of Silence," speaks of creating your own "quiet inner monastery cloister." Yes, silence can be spoken and solitude experienced (to a degree) in the inner person even in the midst of a noisy outer world. Many times I have been in crowded situations and retreated to my inner monastery. A retreat of... and for... the soul.

### The Sanctity

Silence has a way of cleaning up our messes by putting things in perspective. Blaise Pascal, a 17th century French mathematician, physicist, inventor, writer and Christian philosopher, took note of the state of his world and concluded that "all of humanity's problems stem from man's inability to sit quietly in a room alone." Those words deserve serious attention. Perhaps many are afraid to be alone, and afraid to be quiet. To be alone and quiet at the same time can be too much for some to handle. And by fleeing opportunities to be silent they heap upon themselves troubles and problems that otherwise may have been avoided.

But rather than passing judgment on "all of humanity's problems," each of us should focus on his/her own soul first. One of my professors, Dr. David Enyart, was (and I am sure still is) fond of saying, "Your spiritual health is directly related to your ability to live with the questions." And so it is. We need not have every question answered, every riddle solved, every problem unpacked in order to live in the peace that passes all understanding.

The "shalom-shalom" we perpetually need is experienced in just the way Isaiah says it is: "You will keep in perfect peace all who trust in you, whose thoughts are fixed on you!" (26.3, NLT). It is by quietly waiting before God (Psalm 62.5, NLT) that we are given the calm, confident attitude of good cheer that in God's time and in God's way everything is going to be okay. "Be silent (cease striving, be still) and know that I am God" (Psalm 46.10, NLT). Yes, silently seeking God, sitting before God, waiting upon God, trusting in God is God's own prescription for living a life of peace in a place of paradoxes.

Thomas Merton, the most well-known of the monks at Gethsemani, insightfully wrote: "Contradictions have always existed in the soul of man. But it is only when we prefer analysis to silence that they become a constant and insoluble problem. We are not meant to resolve all contradictions but to live with them and rise above them and see them in the light of exterior and objective values which make them trivial by comparison. Silence, then, belongs to the substance of sanctity. In silence and hope are formed the strength of the Saints" (*Thoughts in Solitude,* p. 91).

## The Sanctuary

I have attempted to bring the sanctity of silence back with me to the church I serve. Once a month, on the last Sunday of the month at 6:00 in the evening, the dimly lit sanctuary of Norton Christian Church in Norton, Virginia, is set apart for such a time. We enter in silence. We sit or kneel in silence. We read in silence. We sing in silence. We pray in silence. We listen in silence. We leave in silence.

It is a moving experience for souls who seek a deeper, quieter walk with God. And what better place than the sanctuary, that sanctified space for the worship of God, to experience this? Here is where we sing ancient hymns of faith and contemporary songs of praise, where we celebrate the Sacraments, where we teach the Word, where we recite the creeds and pray the prayers, where we keep Sunday sacred by gathering as the Lord's Family, on the Lord's Day, at the Lord's Table, for the Lord's Glory. Surely the sounds of silence should dwell in the Sanctuary.

*In the silence of the Sanctuary, my soul*
*retreats to pray.*
*I hear the holy hush, I choose*
*no words to say.*

*The sacred silence cleanses me of*
*foolish, trivial nonsense,*
*and washes from my spirit the*
*residue of pretense.*

*In the silence of the Sanctuary,*
*I enter seeking peace,*
*my mind looks for rest, and*
*my worries need release.*

*The thousand thoughts of my inner man*
*begin to fade away,*
*as do the noise and clatter of the*
*crowded, busy day.*

*In the silence of the Sanctuary,*
*unspoken words I hear;*
*the warnings of the Prophets, the Psalmist's*
*joys and tears.*

*The longings of the faithful, crying*
*"what and when and why?"*
*I hear the Good News of Great Joy,*
*"Take courage, it is I."*

*In the silence of the Sanctuary,*
*I hear the ancient voices,*
*and share their sacred hymns,*
*in which my heart rejoices.*

*I hear the communion of the saints,*
*the echoes of their praise.*
*I hear their whispers and their cries from*
*past and present days.*

*In the silence of the Sanctuary, with my Lord*
*I sit alone.*
*I still myself before Him; He makes His*
*presence known.*

*As I linger long with Him, He bids me to*
*draw near,*
*and I grow in understanding...*
*"silence spoke here."*

*~James M. Wells*

# Come and Dine

☩

*Chapter 3*

Greg Sergent

The Bardstown retreat is a deliberate "coming apart" of busy ministers to a place of quiet rest, worship and fellowship. It helps me to refocus and recalibrate my ministry, but more importantly, my life. As a spiritual discipline of retreat, it is my soul care!

I believe we need retreats for our spiritual vitality and formation. Jesus knew the load would get heavy and our toils would leave us feeling frazzled. So His invitation stands today, as it did for his disciples, "Come unto me all who labor and are heavy laden, and I will give you rest" (Matthew 11.28). I imagine John the Beloved, as we often see him depicted in religious art, leaning into Jesus' open arms. Christ's nearness is rest for the soul. You cannot help but rest. "His burden is easy and His yoke is light." Communing with Jesus is the "retreat of the soul" in its purest form.

I realized a few years ago, after returning home from an exhausting week-long "so called" vacation, that I needed something more than the typical American beach trip. I needed a retreat of the soul. When the soul retreats to this sanctuary, surpassing peace stills the heart with an inner tranquility. This is the heart of contemplative spirituality, that finds its deepest satisfaction in the awareness of Christ's presence.

I must admit, one of my favorite activities with the Bardstown brothers is our eating together the more than adequate meal at the convent. Maybe it is my Baptist heritage that equates Christian fellowship with food, but our conversations seem a bit more flavorful and soul-satisfying when seated together at the table.

A casual survey of the life of Jesus through the Gospels reveals that much of his ministry involved eating meals with others. Jesus frequented wedding parties, social gatherings in his honor, a loaves and fish banquet, intimate meals with friends, a seaside breakfast with the disciples and the most intense meal, the Last Supper.

The Last Supper was no ordinary meal. It was Passover history on the cusp of fulfilling redemptive prophecy. In the Passover remembrance, Jesus reminded the disciples that they should remember His broken body and shed blood, and their place as covenant children. Jesus was the new Passover.

The Lord's Table is holy, being set apart to both recall and reflect. And our place and seat at the table has not been forgotten. Jesus eagerly awaits us at the table to share as a covenant family. The table is rightly revered as Holy Communion. Jesus swings the door wide and bids us to "come and dine."

### A Meal to Remember

There are very few natural meals I can remember, even though I have sat at tables garnished with numerous culinary delights. Jesus' memorial meal was simple -- bread and the cup -- but it spans a long tradition of the church for 2000 years. As a family celebration with a long-standing tradition, the meal itself invites "contemplation" as a reflective memorial of His covenant, teachings, life, passion, death and ultimately His resurrection. We remember Jesus! This simple act exhibits the profound staying power of the spiritual reality that touches the core of our being.

Communion is deeply personal, yet at the same time it shapes the corporate identity of the covenant community. Family members of the Redeemer pause together in prayer, break bread, then eat together the sacramental meal. The height, depth, width and breadth of God's gracious favor is surveyed and found infinite. Mystery surrounds the sacred symbol.

As we sit at the Lord's Table, we sense the tension these disciples experienced at the meal. We quietly reflect, savoring every moment, while at the same time the heart wants to leap for joy and remember Christ's wonderful love. It leads the heart in humility and gratitude for God's gracious gift of salvation through His death and resurrection. It serves as a renewal of the heart in covenant with Christ.

The celebration of the Eucharist is the natural symbol of the dynamic spiritual union between Christ and believers. Being his covenant children, rescued from the fall, we are adopted in the family. We cry out, "Abba Father." Christ is our very spiritual sustenance – our "meat and drink."

In communion we enjoy intimate fellowship with Him. In taking the bread we remember that His body was bruised and broken for our transgressions, that

He carried the weight of our sin and alienation. In drinking the cup we remember that He drank the bitter cup of suffering -- the awful dregs of shame. The price for us was His very life's blood. He bought us from sin's slave market, and emancipated us from the power of sin. He bought us "as is," sprinkling His blood at heaven's mercy seat. The purchase was a "once and for all" shedding of His blood -- the elements of the New Covenant.

We experience the sacred in the common activity of breaking bread and sharing drink. In reverence of Jesus, our multiplied pardon, and Christ's imputed righteousness to us, we joyfully sing of grace that is "amazing." We celebrate with confident assurance our certain victory. His life-giving Spirit not only indwells us, but brings the family to the table as one. Indeed, the redeemed ones have cause to sing and celebrate together!

So, in the joy of the Lord, we depart, singing a hymn and looking forward to the meal that will one day be shared with Christ at the heavenly table.

### Contemplative Prayer

What is remembered at the table becomes the breath of that intimate, ongoing fellowship with Christ in prayer. Fellowship is the practical expression of Paul's compelling plea to "pray without ceasing" (1 Thessalonians 5.17). It is a lifestyle conscious of the living presence of Christ within and among us, so that we walk in communion with Him in the midst of everyday life. This is the nature of "contemplative" prayer as noted in previous chapters.

Prayer is the heart laid in abandonment on the throne room altar -- minute by minute. It is indeed a safe place for our hearts. Christ leads us hand in hand to Abba Father where we find grace and mercy. Being "seated in heavenly places," the throne room is the destination of contemplative prayer. It is the invitation of heaven's kingdom come. It is the heartfelt desire for heaven's will on earth.

Prayer is an eternal treasure of praise, silence, thanksgiving, awe, worship, listening, intercession and supplication but most of all, sweet communion. Herein lies the contemplative's greatest joy -- being with Christ. So communion is "being with" Christ, as Christ is one with the Father. What is displayed in the physical meal is the dynamic and awareness of an ongoing eternal spiritual reality: fellowship unbroken! Prayer is the vehicle of transport. It is the retreat of the soul. It is finding rest in the heart of the Father and the awareness of His abiding presence in all of life. This was the dynamic of Jesus' example in prayer.

There are many remarkable aspects about the life of Jesus. As a communicator, His words pierced hearts and captivated minds, as in the Sermon on the Mount. Coupled with His works, His life was magnetic, and His message mystified devoted followers and detractors alike. However, prayer was the compelling and mysterious dynamic of Jesus' life and influence.

Although He was very active in doing ministry, He remained in constant communion with the Father. Yet Jesus would often steal away for concentrated times of quiet reflection. His followers were drawn to the fact that His "private world" was ordered by prayer. The disciples probed the Lord about prayer, imploring, "Lord, teach us to pray!"

Prayer, then, is more than an activity we do, but it is the "inhale and exhale" of life in God. The breath of spiritual life is communion with Jesus. Like breathing, contemplative prayer becomes second nature. Prayer is the ceaseless activity of the spiritual life and the awareness of uninterrupted communion. It is like the natural flow of life from the vine to the branches: an abiding fellowship with Jesus. This was Jesus' example of communion with the Father.

Contemplative prayer as fellowship recognizes that all of life belongs to the Creator of life. It is interesting that there is a cultural struggle today over the question, "Does prayer have a public place in the larger secular culture?" Are boundaries needed, so that prayer and religious expressions remain private?

For Jesus, prayer was in the mainstream of His life. There was no struggle between the so-called secular and sacred. All of life was sacred and an acceptable arena where communion with the Father was lived out. Another way of saying this is there was no secular life for Jesus. Nothing was set aside and reserved for Himself only, or off-limits to the Father and heaven's kingdom. All aspects of Jesus' life were given to the Father, His will and purpose.

St. Anselm of Canterbury describes the all-pervasive presence in contemplation: "Wherever we are, we live, move, and are in Him; whilst also we have Him within us. But, returning from the beatitude that is to be, do thou with the eye of contemplation consider for a while the abundance of grace wherewith He hath enriched thee even in this fleeting life."

In the cultural context, Jesus often prayed for others in public places. However, his example in prayer stood in stark contrast with the religious elite's misuse of prayer. Dramatic public displays of religious right-eousness, rather than authentic communion with the Father, were repulsive and hypocritical. Jesus abhorred duplicitous living, parading prayer as a religious facade that misrepresented His Father and confused flock.

Following in the steps of Jesus leads to a rich spiritual reservoir of the life of the Father flowing forth. Jesus, who was as busy as any high-level business executive, fled the demands of ministry and stole away for quiet, contemplative prayer. And in the silence, yes, in the quiet was the alignment of the heart of the Son with the heart of His Father. He relished and practiced the retreat of the soul!

### Eating Together
*The Church is Fellowship*

Believers' communion with Christ is the glue for the community of faith. The early church ate their bread together with singleness of heart. They perceived and remembered the horrific moment of Jesus' death as a far-reaching rescue of love. His love held nail-pierced hands to the rugged crossbeam, and His power enabled resurrection-life.

Likewise, love holds redeemed followers everywhere together as one, and His life is lived out in the echo of his words, "love one another." Kindness, tenderheartedness and forgiveness are all part of the faith community. Make no mistake, meeting Jesus at the cross opens our arms in a loving embrace of one another. So the early church devoted themselves to the apostles' teaching, breaking of bread and prayer (Acts 2.42-47). This fellowship or "koinonia" with one another was compelling evidence that Christ was with them.

We are the church where His life-giving spirit operates. The church moves, grows, serves, loves and advances through the presence of Christ. Anything of eternal significance is only accomplished through the Spirit's empowerment and our soul in retreat with Christ. So, whether you are reflecting on the awe of nature, sitting in silence, meditating upon His Word, interceding in prayer or worshiping through the beauty of Christ-centered liturgy, Jesus is present. Acknowledge His presence, become acutely aware that He is within you and is the vibrancy and life among us. We are the body of Christ.

### Retreat Often

With all our modern technology, we have an urgent sense that time is slipping away. Meaningful life experiences are passing us by. We are missing so much, we feel. In panic, we chase every passing fad that speeds before us. We are simply too busy and distracted for the retreat of the soul or even fellowship with believers -- at least, we think we are. And without such a retreat our life is held hostage to surface level living. Without deep trenches to the soul, spiritual dryness and famish hold us captive to living for what we see, feel and touch.

In a perpetual neglect of the soul, we draw from the world's empty wells and drink from broken cisterns. As a result our lives remain empty and unsatisfied. Christ invites us to a much better way of living. He offers living water, both refreshing and satisfying to the soul. Even more, He has saved us a place at His banquet table and invites us to "come and dine."

Retreat! Retreat often to the sanctuary of God! Your deepest longings are satisfied in His presence at His table. Then, along with the Psalmist, proclaim, "Oh taste and see that the Lord is good!"

☩

*For I have received from the Lord that which also I delivered unto you, That the Lord Jesus the same night in which he was betrayed took bread:*

*And when he had given thanks, he broke it, and said, Take, eat: this is my body, which is broken for you: this do in remembrance of me.*

*After the same manner also he took the cup, when he had sipped, saying, This cup is the new covenant in my blood: this do, as often as you drink it, in remembrance of me.*

*For as often as you eat this bread, and drink this cup, you do show the Lord's death till he comes.*

*I Corinthians 11:23-26 (KJBT)*

# Ritual and Liturgy

✠

*Chapter 4*

Garrett W. Sheldon

I walk into the darkened living room early in the morning, light two small candles on the stone hearth, start some medieval choral church music (Victoria; Tallis; Du Caurroy), open my Bible, read and begin to pray, meditate and listen for God's Spirit. The sermon, or message, or article is then written: quickly, effortlessly as if God's power pours through the fountain pen ink onto the white sheets of paper. Twenty or thirty minutes later the Sunday sermon is finished. It will be revised slightly through written additions and amplified by the Holy Spirit from the pulpit of a small town Baptist church, but the body of the message has been composed, quickly, smoothly, softly, joyfully, because of the ritual practiced behind its composition.

The candlelight and choral music, the silent darkened room, sometimes the scent of fragrant incense, the glow of a fire in the stone fireplace, a special tea at my side and a robe on my back supplement this religious environment. This is the original purpose of church ritual: to place us in a spiritual setting, an otherworldly mood, close to God, conducive to personal devotion far from the ordinary social environment with its inter-ruptions, demands, temptations and distractions. Being with the Lord is our "God Place."

Ritual, settings, "works," (bowing, kneeling, making the sign of the cross, lifting the eyes to heaven) have sometimes been ridiculed as empty, meaningless (or worse, idolatrous) habits, vain gestures and repetitions, offensive to a God in Christ who is everywhere and always personal and new. And ritual can certainly become those things: routine, rote, foolish, meaningless and tedious. But religious ritual properly meant (and practiced throughout the Church's history) is designed to usher within the believer a special, holy state, without conformity to the world and human desire.

Christian ritual, in the proper sense, is meant to draw the believer into a deeper relationship with God, to hear and abide in His presence. These actions, meant to foster worship and contemplation, are to bring us closer to the divine, and everyone has such rituals of some sort. It is an acknowledgement that we are weak and often have difficulty "getting up" a spiritual state of mind; we need a familiar ritual to bring us into that meditative, contemplative state. Ritual in this sense is not formal and prideful but a humble recognition of our need for support for our prayer.

My ritual -- what helps me to remove myself from the world and my petty thoughts and concerns and focus on the majesty and wonder of God, the mystery of the Almighty and His purposes and ways -- comes out of my upbringing in the Anglo-Catholic Episcopal Church, the "High Church" branch of the American Anglican or English Church. When I grew up in Wisconsin in the 1950s, this was the predominant expression of the U.S. Church of England, affected by the Oxford Movement of the nineteenth century that sought to restore many Catholic practices and doctrines to that early Protestant church in Britain. My family has been associated with that denomination for centuries, including the Archbishop of Canterbury during the Restoration of the 17th Century. Many priests, bishops and musicians in the church are in my family lineage and probably influence my spiritual sensibilities.

The emphasis on the Mass or Eucharist (also called the Lord's Supper), ancient creeds and prayers, chants and motions, kneeling, bowing, and the sign of the cross infuse these rituals and culture. Aesthetics of gothic stone buildings, organ music and choral singing, incense, candles, bells, stained glass windows, Christian images, sanctuaries of shadows, quiet and peace, clergy vestments and positions, all contributed to the sense of mystery, reverence and meditation.

As a child I found all this rather spooky and odd -- so unlike the busy, loud, bustling-city on the outside of the cathedral. But even at a young age, when I hardly understood it, it gave me a sense of the dignity, awesomeness and solemnity of God. I may not have heard much of the Gospel preached or been taught Christian morals beyond the Commandments and modeled behavior, but the elevated language and sophisticated manner of this environment made an indelible impression on me. I imbued a deep sense of the Holy, the wonder and goodness of God. The Lord conveyed in this atmosphere is both fearful and gentle, powerful and loving, majestic and protective. A sense of God's greatness, care, provision, power and protection embraced me in this environment.

I have often heard similar impressions expressed by believers growing up in the Roman Catholic Church, viewing it as a rock of stability, security and protection in a volatile, dangerous, unpredictable world -- a place of peace and comfort, continuity and hope. This is why many traditional Catholics resist change, even when it might be of Jesus and His Spirit, who is always new and unpredictable. That is why, when I replicate this atmosphere in my home sanctuary (candlelight, music, incense, quiet solitude, subdued light) I return to that mindset of meditation and holiness.

I realize that most Protestants find much of this strange, even disturbing. These traditional practices and associations may seem stiff and formal, foreign and unnatural. But most Christian denominations have some kind of ritual, practice or habit with which they associate faith, worship, prayer and meditation.

They enter a "spiritual space" or their "prayer closet" somewhere, somehow. It may be certain music, rooms, or pictures, or outside in nature (where I also find inspiration). Some find images, certain kinds of gatherings, devotional writings, evangelists or worship styles inspiring. Bible classes, meals, fellowship and discussions may also be familiar rituals associated with the Christian faith. The important thing is acknow-ledging that prayer and contemplation may not always have to be spontaneous, "fresh," free and different to be real; set forms may actually contribute to meditation, worship and religious experience. Routine may become routine and stale, boring and trivial, but it may also provide comfort and stimulate spiritual feelings and growth. How often God has given me an insight, a peace, during such "quiet times." Quiet times may energize, stimulating action for Christ!

I am now a minister in the "free" church, the Southern Baptist, after first joining my wife's Presbyterian Church and then participating in modern Episcopal, Methodist, Pentecostal and others. The "free" church started in Europe, free from both the State and from set rituals, liturgies and governance. Its emphasis on the Bible and the free flow of the Holy Spirit in worship, as well as congregational autonomy (without bishops, hierarchy, presbyteries, etc.) was meant to avoid the dead ritual without life.

A preaching of the Gospel as alive, applied to everyday life, spread the faith during the Protestant era. I saw the power of this in the "In Touch" ministry of Charles Stanley and was called by God to this tradition. The Catholic Church, as well as other denominations, are now integrating some of this free church emphasis on the Scriptures, daily Christian living and congregational self-government. My background now makes me very ecumenical, appreciating all traditions. The Church to me combines a reverence for the richness of the past, an emphasis on the Bible and on preaching and an openness to the Holy Spirit.

### Liturgy

This leads to the place of Liturgy, or planned, ordered, standardized worship, prayer and ceremony. The Oxford English Dictionary simply defines "liturgy" as "a set form of public worship" -- an orderly, planned, predictable, disciplined, reliable structure to worship, prayer and contemplation. The church service liturgy I grew up with began with entering a quiet, dark, reverent place, with scents and sounds of generations of believers. It was a culture of faith from the Anglican

31

"Book of Common Prayer," the English language version of the Catholic missal going back centuries in church history: prayers and practices refined by hundreds of the faithful and ministering to thousands in times of need, grief, confusion and helplessness. The 1928 Prayer Book I grew up with had hardly changed since the first edition in the 1600s (it was substantially revised in the 1970s, with so much of our changing culture). The dignity and grace, poetry and profundity of the original Book of Common Prayer, like the King James Version Bible of the same era, was at times difficult to understand, so it was "updated" to contemporary language to make it more accessible to modern people. The beauty and majesty of the old book must somehow relate to current times, preserving the glory and richness of the past.

Such an "order of worship" is designed to draw one into a spiritual, godly attitude: reverent and holy, meditative and attentive, contemplative. It is also designed to preserve and convey certain essentials of the faith (Psalms, Gospels, Commandments, Lord's Prayer, Apostles Creed, etc.) every Sunday, to keep that center of the faith alive.

The purpose of Mass or Eucharist or the Lord's Supper is to reenact the suffering and death of Jesus on the cross. It reminds us that God sacrificed His Son, a man without sin, for our sins, and that He took the punishment and penalty our sin deserves -- death and hell -- and made it possible, by faith, for our sins to be forgiven, and for us to spend eternity in heaven with a perfect God and have a piece of heaven within us now by the indwelling Holy Spirit that resides within believers. That reuniting of our relationship with God, broken by our disobedience, is the center of our Christian faith and should be reenacted every Sunday. It is a reminder of the essentials of our faith.

Special liturgies, or ordinances or sacraments, are designed for special occasions in which God makes something sacred or holy: baptism, marriage, ordination, burial. Even contemporary wedding ceremonies borrow from the *Solemnization of Holy Matrimony* liturgy in the Book of Common Prayer. Its opening statement is familiar, detailing the origin and purpose of Christian marriage:

> Dearly beloved, we are gathered together here in the sight of God and in the face of this company, to join together this man and this woman in holy matrimony; which is an honorable estate, instituted of God, signifying unto us the mystical union that is betwixt Christ and His Church.... and therefore is not by any to be entered into unadvisedly or lightly; but reverently, discreetly, advisedly, soberly, and in the fear of God.

This is quite different from a superficial, emotional, purely social wedding ceremony that focuses on the people involved, their needs, their love, and so on. The ancient prayers of traditional liturgy focus on God and His purposes, laws and ways. They come from centuries of thoughtful, prayerful theology, practice, experience and devotion of godly people.

Consequently, I have perceived a depth to these ceremonial prayers that is often missing in more

porary "relevant" services, and I have seen an
iation of their beauty and profoundness. Often,
traditional wedding or funeral in my evangelical
church, I have heard people express how meaningful it
was. Similarly, the funeral service in the traditional
liturgy conveys a depth and comfort often missing in
more loosely constructed formats.

The familiar words at the gravesite summarize the
meaning of a Christian's death: "Unto Almighty God we
commend the soul of our dear brother departed, and we
commit his body to the ground, earth to earth, ashes to
ashes, dust to dust; in the sure and certain hope of the
Resurrection unto eternal life, through our Lord, Jesus
Christ."

The English liturgy contains many beautiful and
meaningful prayers for those mourning the death of a
loved one, refined over centuries of experience and
faith, giving hope to those grieving. One of my favorites,
which I often read over the casket at the conclusion of
the funeral service, making the sign of the cross over the
body of the deceased: "Depart O Christian soul, unto
God the Father who created thee; God the Son who
redeemed thee; and God the Spirit who sanctified thee."

Another prayer that holds special meaning to me, as it
was prayed over me as a boy, is the blessing for a
birthday, which was given over the children every
month for those born in that month and which I have
adapted for my blessing of the children in my Baptist
church before they go off to children's church. At St.
Paul's Episcopal Church in Milwaukee, Wisconsin, we
would kneel at the altar rail as the priest said: "Watch
over thy child, O Lord, as his days increase; bless and

guide him wherever he may be, keeping him unspotted from the world. Strengthen him when he stands, comfort him when discouraged or sorrowful; raise him up if he fall; and in his heart may thy peace which passeth understanding, abide all the days of his life, through Jesus Christ our Lord, Amen."

I have adapted this children's prayer, varying it a bit every Sunday, as I pray over the children in the church as they go off to their Children's Church. It is a blessing. I see their responses: heads bowed, hands clasped in prayer, taking it in, as I did sixty years ago, feeling God's love and provision, help and protection, awesomeness and peace.

Finally, a reason for drawing upon Liturgy is to avoid the subjectivism that is easy for any minister to fall into. As busy, often harried, tired pastors, we find it easy to bring our own personal issues to prayer and worship, substituting our own thoughts and concerns for God's Truth. Liturgy brings us back to God, grounds us in His Word, over and above our weak, temporal lives. It, like ritual, provides a discipline and order we need in this frantic, fallen world of ours. Either ritual or liturgy can become empty and meaningless, routine and dead. But combined with the Holy Spirit of God which they are meant to usher in, they can be a great blessing to us and our ministry.

✠

*Blessed is the man who does not walk in the counsel of the ungodly, nor stands in the way of sinners, nor sits in the seat of the scornful.*

*But his delight is in the law of the Lord; and in his law does he meditate day and night.*

*And he shall be like a tree planted by the rivers of water, that brings forth its fruit in its season; its leaf also shall not wither; and whatever he does shall prosper.*

*The ungodly are not so: but are like the chaff which the wind drives away.*

*Therefore the ungodly shall not stand in the judgment, nor sinners in the congregation of the righteous.*

*For the Lord knows the way of the righteous: but the way of the ungodly shall perish.*

*Psalm 1 (KJBT)*

# Biblical Meditation

✠

*Chapter 5*

James M. Wells

"But his delight is in the law of the LORD,
and on his law he meditates day and night."
Psalm 1.2, NIV

We have Pastor's Prayer Groups in the Church I serve. Four groups are praying as of this writing. Each group consists of three to five souls, and each group meets for twelve Sundays with one purpose in mind: to learn to pray the will of God by praying the Word of God. This is my working definition of biblical meditation.

Biblical meditation is a natural ingredient in the practice of the contemplative life. As mentioned in chapter one, the contemplative life is a practical expression of Paul's teaching to "pray without ceasing." *It is a lifestyle of conscious living in the presence of God and walking in communion with Him in the midst of everyday life.*

Brother Lawrence, the 17th Century French Monk, no doubt meditated as he "practiced the presence of God" (the contemplative life) in his daily activities. So it stands to reason that for one to pray and live contemplatively he must meditate on God's Word.

## Biblical Meditation

Much has been written by saints and scholars on *meditation* and *contemplation*. Much effort has been made by great thinkers and practitioners of prayer to define, explain and distinguish the two, and I have endeavored to understand these fine nuances. These nuances are so nearly indistinguishable that meditation and contemplation are often used interchangeably. One can dissect meditation and contemplation to the point that there is nothing left to use. I will not attempt to swim in those deep waters of distinction. They are two sides of the proverbial same coin. So, using the old adage "too much analysis leads to paralysis" as a guide, here we go. We begin with the question. . .

## What is Biblical Meditation?

Greater minds and souls than mine have given definitions and descriptions of biblical meditation. Christian meditation is "an active thought process whereby we give ourselves to the study of the Word, praying over it and asking God to give us understanding by the Spirit."

Robert Morgan writes, "Biblical meditation is the powerful practice of pondering, personalizing and practicing Scripture" (*Reclaiming the Lost Art of Biblical Meditation,* p. x). It is "the habit that allows us to pause long enough to be still and to know that God is God".

Thomas Merton, 20th century American monk, wrote in *Spiritual Direction and Meditation*, "To meditate is to exercise the mind in serious reflection." (p. 52). When giving this short definition, Merton put in place a foundation upon which he built a more comprehensive structure to explain more precisely his concept of biblical meditation. His small book is a must-read and you will find yourself returning to it time and again.

Now, of course, we must give attention to the Hebrew verb pronounced *hagah.* It means to "growl, groan, sigh, mutter, or speak," and from that it has come to mean to meditate, to ponder, to ruminate. As Franz Delitzsch further describes, meditation signifies "the quiet soliloquy of one who is searching and thinking." William Wilson (*Wilson's Old Testament Word Studies,* p. 271) says that to meditate "implies what we express by one talking to himself." The Bible actually encourages talking to one's self, but that is a matter for another time.

An analogy often used in describing biblical meditation is "to chew the cud," the idea being to chew and re-chew the Word of God in order to absorb the necessary nutrients. This practice leads to a contemplative and obedient life. In meditating on God's Word we listen for God's voice; we listen for "the whispers of God" (Richard Foster, *Sanctuary of the Soul,* p. 83). And, as mentioned in chapter two, silence can be an invaluable aid as we listen for God's whispers.

### Meditation in the Bible

Richard Foster writes, "In Biblical times people were well versed in how to meditate; it was the air they breathed" (*Sanctuary of the Soul,* p. 60). It seems that we have difficulty breathing this air today, for reasons I will not attempt to name here. But, for our instruction, Scripture records examples of biblical meditation.

Isaac "went out to the field one evening to *meditate*..." (Genesis 24.63, NIV). What was going on in his life that necessitated such an endeavor? He was seeking God's will in a serious matter. The chief of the household servants had been sent on a mission by his father, Abraham, to find him a wife. This was a serious matter indeed and worthy of seeking the will of God.

Joshua admonishes the people, "Do not let this Book of the Law depart from your mouth; *meditate* on it day and night, so that you may be careful to do everything written in it. Then you will be prosperous and successful" (Joshua 1.8, NIV). Note the connection between knowing the Word of God and doing the will of God! Meditating on God's Word will lead us to do God's will.

David prayed, "May the words of my mouth and the *meditation* of my heart be pleasing in your sight..." (Psalm 19.14, NIV). What a powerfully biblical thing to pray!

David also told God, "I lie awake thinking of you, *meditating* on you through the night" (Psalm 63.6, NLT). Did David, a man after God's own heart, deliberately stay awake at night to ponder the majesty and the mysteries of Yahweh? So it seems. And, no doubt, during the nights when sleep would not come David meditated on His Shepherd and positioned himself to hear His voice. What better way to spend one's time! We see similar words in Psalm 119.148: "My eyes stay open through the watches of the night, that I may *meditate* on your promises" (NIV).

Asaph wrote, "I will *meditate* on all your works and consider all your mighty deeds" (Psalm 77.12, NIV). This is a good thing to do when you feel overwhelmed by difficult situations. One of the "mighty deeds" Asaph meditated on was the parting of the Red Sea -- not a bad thing to meditate on. In fact, Psalm 77 as a whole should be carefully and prayerfully read and reread. God may shout something to you, or He may whisper.

Paul writes, "Finally, brothers, whatever is true, whatever is noble, whatever is right, whatever is pure, whatever is lovely, whatever is admirable—if anything is excellent or praiseworthy—think about such things" (Philippians 4.8, NIV). The Greek word "think" also means "to reason, to reckon, to dwell on." Paul, a studious man, knew the value of meditating on all things good and noble. And, of course, he knew that God's Word was the best and noblest of all.

Paul says, "Set your minds on things above, not on earthly things" (Colossians 3.2, NIV). "To set" also means "to exercise the mind, to savor." We can clearly see the meaning of meditation in Paul's words to the Colossians.

Paul, encouraging young Timothy in his pastoral duties, told him to *"meditate* upon these things" (1 Timothy 4.15, KJV). "These things" included teachings about apostasy, avoiding godless myths, training himself to be godly, putting his hope in the living God, setting an example for the believers under his care and giving attention to the public reading of Scripture and to preaching and teaching. Paul was saying, "Yes, Timothy,

41

'meditate upon these things,' for you have been given great responsibilities."

Biblical meditation was, indeed, the air God's people breathed. And for the contemporary Christian, it can be a breath of fresh air in an age of all kinds of worldly pollution. Praying God's Word in order to do God's will is a God-blessed spiritual undertaking which results in a life that glorifies God.

## Motivations for Meditation

The Psalms compose the prayer book of Israel and the Church. They are God's voice to us, and our voice to God. It is said that "we were born with this book in our very bones" (Andre Chouraqui).

The first Psalm reveals a basic and essential motivation for biblical meditation.

*Blessed is the man who does not walk in the counsel of the wicked or stand in the way of sinners or sit in the seat of mockers. But his delight is in the law of the LORD, and on his law he meditates day and night (Psalm 1.1-2, NIV).*

Delighting IN and meditating ON God's Word are the keys to understanding this wisdom psalm. God's Word positions us to live a life blessed by God, described in verse 6 as "the way of the righteous." This stands in contrast with "the way of the wicked" who reject God's words (Psalm 50.17). The righteous take delight, find pleasure in, and see the value of God's Word, and therefore make it a matter of habitual meditation.

We see a similar truth in Psalm 119.97: "Oh, how I *love* your law! I *meditate* on it all day long." Love for God's Word also motivates meditation. Merton says, "One who really meditates does not merely think, he also loves" (*Spiritual Direction and Meditation*, p. 52). A deep and abiding love for God and His Word is the motivation for meditation for the "way of the righteous."

The righteous know the power and authority of God's Word, and understand that the best way to pray for God's will to be done is by praying God's Word. After all, it is a lamp to show us the righteous way (Psalm 119.105) and it keeps us from wandering down the wicked way (Psalm 119.11).

These truths have fashioned my personal definition of biblical meditation which I mentioned in the first paragraph: praying the Word of God in order to do the will of God.

Now while the focus here is Psalm 1, all of the Psalms are fertile fields for meditation. They are not "abstract treatises on the divine nature" says Merton, but rather "in them we learn to know God not by analyzing various concepts of His divinity, but by praising and loving Him." The Psalms "only reveal their full meaning to those who use them in order to praise God" (*Praying the Psalms,* p. 19).

Yes, the Psalter provides a steady spiritual diet for souls who wish to pray the will of God by praying the Word of God. Our love FOR God's Word leads us to delight IN God's Word and to meditate ON God's Word. Serendipitously simple!

# Meditation 101

For the soul who may be unsure about where and how to begin, I would suggest praying and meditating on something familiar and comforting. I believe the best passage in the Bible to help a novice begin a life of meditation and contemplative prayer contains what we call "The Lord's Prayer."

The purpose of all prayer is twofold: to give God praise and to seek God's will. Jesus taught His disciples to pray (Matthew 6.9-13):

> (1) Our Father who is in heaven, hallowed be Your name (Giving God praise).
> (2) Your kingdom come, Your will be done on earth as it is in heaven" (Seeking God's will).

The rest of the prayer is petitioning God for His will to be done by:

> (1) Providing for our daily needs (God's provision);
> (2) Granting us forgiveness as we forgive others (God's pardon);
> (3) Delivering us from the evil one and his ways (God's protection).

"The Lord's Prayer" is perfect for meditation, either word for word or thought for thought. One can meditate on one section a day for six days, and then pray and meditate on the prayer as a whole on the seventh day. I like and use this outline to provide structure for my practice of meditation.

## Monday: Praise

Our Father who is in heaven, hallowed be your name.

## Tuesday: Priority

Your kingdom come, Your will be done, on earth as it is in heaven.

## Wednesday: Provision

Give us this day our daily bread.

## Thursday: Pardon

And forgive us our trespasses, as we forgive those who trespass against us.

.

## Friday: Protection

And lead us not into temptation, but deliver us from evil.

## Saturday: Praise

For yours is the kingdom, and the power, and the glory forever. Amen.

## Sunday: The Entire Prayer

## Finally

Carefully and prayerfully consider these 25 verses for meditation: Psalms 1; 8; 13; 23; 27; 42; 46; 51; 62; 100; 121, Proverbs 1.1-7; 3.5,6; Matthew 6.9-13; Romans 6.1-14; I Corinthians 13; Galatians 5.13-26; Ephesians 6.10-20; Philippians 4.4-9; I Thessalonians 4.18; I Timothy 1.12-17; II Timothy 2.8-13; Hebrews 11; James 1.2-7; I Peter 1.3-9.

I hope that this analysis does not cause spiritual paralysis, but rather encourages your practice of the contemplative life. So I now say... *delight* in the Word of God and on his Word *meditate* day and night!

# Nature's Sanctuary

☩

*Chapter 6*

Mitch Estep

"I don't know if I believe in you anymore." These are the words I finally declared to God during a dark night in my soul.

The day of my declaration was cold, as winter was just ending. Much like myself, places on the rock remained frozen and would not thaw until a warmer day. I was deeply depressed and grieving. Nothing that had happened over the previous year and a half made any sense or fit into the narrative I thought should play out. I felt alone.

I was sitting on a giant rock with a flag perched on top of it that overlooks our city. Winter had stripped the trees of their leaves. The birds were all fluffed out. The sky was deep blue fading to orange and pink as the sun was setting to my left.

The tree tops beneath me swayed back and forth with creaks and groans that complained at the winter wind which blew down from the mountain behind me. I was protected within the orange and gray layers of sandstone that stood sentinel over the valley. The crow's call made me jump again and again. I must have been close to its nest.

On that day, I took off my gloves, put my head down and quietly said to God, "I don't know if I believe in you anymore...."

This is also the place I hear from God.

I retreat to this cleft on the left side of Flag Rock on a regular basis. I sit, I think and look out over the peace and quiet of the town and talk to God. It is on that rock that my most honest conversations with God happen. This is where I ask the BIG questions. Where I ask "WHY" questions that have no easy answers. Where I give my "two cents" worth of ignorance to the omniscient Creator of the universe about how He is running things down here. This rock is where I sit when my world goes unsteady and out of kilter. It is where I go when I feel the very ground will swallow me. It is also where I go to worship in quiet ways. To rest and be in God's word. It is where I meet God. It is my sanctuary.

If you sat down with me on that large outcropping of rock, you would see the small stone bowls formed by the dripping of rain and snow on the floor of the cleft. Looking over the edge, fragments of rock at the base are broken out, making the shelf. Layers and colors of stone have been fashioned over time, just as He planned. God reveals something about Himself there to us.

Look at the trees that surround this safe haven -- their tops, 70-100 feet off the forest floor, swaying below us; the trees just taking their time growing and stretching to the heavens, lifting their branches in praise of the Divine Gardener. Poplar and hickory don't grow fast, just a little at a time, up and out; and each year they put on their best green robes to show off the splendor of God. The trees slowly pull nutrients and water to produce their seeds and nuts for the birds and animals that depend on them through the cold winters. God teaches us through the interactions of nature, and the beautiful adornment of nature's sanctuary.

Consider the crows and their obnoxious yelling at us as we sit there disturbing their lives with our presence. They make their nests, solve problems, and raise their chicks. They remember and confront those who infringe upon their territory. What is God saying through the instinctual nature of crows? It is also their sanctuary.

## Nature Reflects God's Character

It is natural for me to go to the mountains. It's where I have always gone to hear from God, to arrange my thoughts and plans, to get my soul in order. From my earliest memories I've loved the mountains and the forests. It's almost like they are in my bones.

Once I was sitting up on a mountain, eating a sandwich under some large hemlock trees. Summer was over, but autumn had not yet set in. The sky was clear. The pine trees and needles all around me smelled delicious. I was looking at these enormous hemlock trunks that have grown for 150 to 200 years. Yes, there are still some places like that. The lowest branches start 50 feet off the ground. I said, "God is like that hemlock tree: strong, majestic, and wild. He is protective against the wind and elements. I can rest in His shade, just like this tree." Then all of a sudden it hit me; God is not like the hemlock. Rather, the hemlock reflects the strength and constancy of God!

We Christians believe that God created the heavens and the earth, and everything in creation was made good and pleasing to Him. It was His voice that spoke things into existence, His imagination that made life a reality, His voice that breathed life across the dark expanses. He put a glimpse of Himself in most everything He made.

To say "God is like the tree" is a very short step from ascribing to the tree divinity. But to say "the tree reflects God" means the tree mirrors the glory of its Creator. It magnifies an attribute that makes God better known to us. That is the ministry of these great watchmen of the forest.

Consider how the movement and action of creation are portrayed in this beautiful picture of the worship of God in their natural sanctuary.

*Let the heavens rejoice, let the earth be glad; let the sea resound, and all that is in it Let the fields be jubilant, and everything in them; let all the trees of the forest sing for joy. Let all creation rejoice before the Lord, for he comes, he comes to judge the earth. He will judge the world in righteousness and the peoples in his faithfulness.*
*(Psalm 96:11-13)*

The trees and the fields, the waves and the sea all rejoice. What strikes me as odd is they are rejoicing over the fact that Lord is coming. He is also faithful and righteous. Creation doesn't argue over this or try to explain it away. No, creation knows the truth and rejoices over it. In fact Paul wrote that all of nature is eagerly expecting His return (Romans 8.19-21).

How much stronger would we grow? How much more jubilant would we act? How much more loudly would our voices resound? How much more at peace would we be? How much more confident could we become with the master of our souls if we worshiped God eagerly, knowing He is always present?

There is a pond next to the office where I work. It was a river years ago, but it was changed and rerouted so that now it is a pond with a retaining dam at each end. There are trees along both sides, along with houses and duplexes. It is over a mile long. Fish fill its waters. Turtles raise their heads out of the depths for air. Fountains keep the waters alive and fresh. And even though it has changed, it still reveals God's glory.

God is not only Creator of life, but sustainer. He meets the needs of every situation, sustaining life and empowering it to flourish, even when there is disturbance. There is also mystery here. Hundreds of years of travelers had journeyed on that river before it was changed. We don't know what lies within those waters, only its outward beauty. The Glory of God is reflected in its surface, and mysteries are hidden in its shallow depths.

He is here. The woods and nature instinctively draw our attention to Him. They are permeated with His qualities and desires. It's hard to think of other things besides God when confronted with His creation. And it's not so much that we are thinking about Him directly, but that we are alive to Him – our souls innately open to His presence. We are aware of Him, like we are aware of the sun on our backs, the breeze on our skin, and the smell of rich loam under our feet.

We need places like this, where we can sit, contemplate, learn and hear what God is saying to us. It's easy to get off track in life -- to be drawn away by the distractions and noise of life. Our souls need to get away into silence and solitude, where God can restore and reorient us onto the pathways of His design (Isaiah 48:17).

## God's Idea

This is not a new idea, or a mystical idea. Nature's sanctuary is God's idea. This is where we as people have always gone to find God and commune with Him. In fact, you could argue it was God's preference from the very beginning. He placed Adam and Eve in a garden full of trees and animals. He walked in nature's first sanctuary with Adam in the cool of the evening. At times like that, His speaking is normal, natural, and healing.

The book of Job, the oldest writing we have in the Judeo-Christian faith, draws our attention to the created world. Job's friend, Elihu, goes into a long speech about knowing God. He says in chapter 37, "Listen to this, Job; stop and consider God's wonders" (Job 37.14). Stop and consider this. He gives examples of clouds, rain and snow that cannot be explained. He also suggests God's voice is like thunder, and His breath is an icy wind that makes animals cower and take shelter. At times like this, God's speaking can be overwhelming.

The words of Paul ring true throughout time and make it plain to all humanity:

*What may be known about God is plain to them, <u>because</u> God has made it plain to them. For since the creation of the world God's invisible qualities—His eternal power and divine nature—have been clearly seen, being understood from what has been made, so that people are without excuse.*
*(Romans 1.19-20)*

At those moments, God's speaking is to everyone.

At times God's speech is slow and patient, as He teaches us and we learn. Moses spent forty years in the wilderness and in solitude, as God prepared him to become the greatest leader in Israel's history, a method God used to train many leaders throughout history. Moses then gave the Israelite nation the opportunity to spend time with God in the wilderness, away from everything they knew, so they could focus on worshiping Him and receiving His Word. We know they turned away from Him and fashioned a golden calf to worship. God then led them into another wilderness for years as an opportunity to train up their children to follow Him and become warriors and worshipers. His words in the wilderness sometimes correct and rebuke.

## God Still Speaks

As I sat in the cleft of his hands overlooking that valley, God's speech was gentle and compassionate. He responded to my soul's weeping and exclamation of disbelief with a simple sentence, *"It doesn't change the fact that I'm here."*

In that simple response I heard so much more. I heard:

*I am here reflected in what you
touch, see, hear, and smell.
I am known because of the cold rock protecting you.
I am seen as the sun paints the sky with
my brushes of light and hope.
I am here when life is beautiful and calm.
I am here when life goes dark and chaotic.
I AM HERE!*

Nothing you can say or do or believe will change the simple fact that I am here.

We all have our unique or difficult ways about us, our dark times with inexplicable questions; it's part of being human. But God can speak through nature right to our distinctly peculiar need so that we hear Him. In our sorrow He suffers with us; in our exuberance, He sings with us. In our struggles He can strengthen and cheer us on. What He says to us is sometimes familiar, and can be understood by others. At other times, our need or desire is so great that He may have to use a unique voice to get us to hear.

But, ALWAYS, *God is here.*

Nothing can separate us from the piercing presence of our 'Abba-Father' (Romans 8.19, 38-39). When we venture into the silence of the wilderness with Him we can open ourselves up to the presence of His Holy Spirit. It's a place where our souls come alive, vibrant and accessible to God. When we sit in the beautiful sanctuary of clouded ceilings and swaying columns, the musical choir of the earth fills our bones with their choruses. His character is reflected through all He created. His divine nature is glimpsed within the random flight of a butterfly, the songs that rise from a stream rolling over stones and the lights of the cosmos twinkling in a moonless night. Here God is able to sing His song to us and within us. Here He can refine our marching orders. Here He reveals the untamed nature of His character and will. Here He can make us alive with His word and presence.

It might be like the churning of water over pebbles. It might be in the decomposing soft pulp of a fallen tree. He could use the whirlwind or the storm. He could softly hum to us in the rhythm of a bird's flight. However God communicates, it is to change us, shape us, refine us and polish us to reflect His glory and beauty.

*If we wander there in worship, He welcomes us.*
*If we stumble into the wilderness to pray,*
*He intercedes with us.*
*If we journey there for counsel, He speaks to us.*
*If we venture out for sanctification, He molds us.*
*If we kneel before Him in repentance, He forgives us.*

As the Lord told Israel, concerning their hearts, "I will lead [you] into the wilderness, and speak tenderly to [you]" (Hosea 2.14).

When our souls feel dark and winter has set into our hearts let Him lead us to His sanctuary. God has put himself into the creation of this world and the salvation of His people. He has given us His breath of life. He has placed around us examples that reflect His character,

His untamed nature and brilliance. The Father has quietly spoken into existence His heart for us to see and learn from. It only makes sense that He would speak through it. It is logical that the one who gave us His Spirit would make Himself heard. He speaks in the most natural places, in the most distinct ways. He dialogues in the language of our unique circumstances and peculiar personalities.

Make time for getting into nature; in fact, make it a priority! Allow yourself the freedom to regularly separate from the world. Quietly remove the distractions of life and allow God to speak to you. Stand in the cleft of His goodness, on the solid rock of the Scripture -- His Word. Look all around at His creation and marvel at His splendor, rejoice in His promises and bask in His presence. After all, our circumstances do not change the simple fact that He is here and He is speaking.

The God of grace will speak to your soul, revealing Himself in the beauty of His sanctuary -- nature. Hear His desire as you walk in communion with your Father in the beauty of His world.

*This is my Father's world:*
*The birds their carols raise,*
*The morning light, the lily white,*
*Declare their Maker's praise.*
*This is my Father's world:*
*He shines in all that's fair;*
*In the rustling grass I hear Him pass,*
*He speaks to me everywhere.*

*~Maltbie Babcock*

# Prayers from the Path

✠

*Chapter 7*

Carl Roudebush

When I think of the contemplative life of a believer I usually envision sitting in a quiet, secluded place, without thought of time and in privacy from the world around us. Being able to spend time in reflection, examination and openness to the presence of God sometimes feels like a luxury. However, being open and receptive to the leading and prompting of the Holy Spirit and God's Word is a necessity.

As we look at the lives and circumstances of several people in the Scripture, we sometimes do not see this picture of serenity and solitude. Certainly Jesus sought out and exercised these moments throughout His earthly ministry -- those quiet times away from the crowds and even His closest followers. They had to hunt for Him to try to understand what he was doing and to learn the lessons of His times alone with the heavenly Father. He had to teach them to pray as He prayed. We, or at least I, do not always seem to find these quiet moments of contemplation and separation from the pressure and interruptions of life.

As I think about being afforded the luxury of time to think, reflect and contemplate God's will, I am reminded of those many times when a phone call comes in the middle of the night and I find myself in the car racing to the hospital or emergency room or home where tragedy has struck. My mind runs away as I picture what I might encounter  when I get there. How should I react? What should I say, or not say? How can I be God's presence to those in the crisis? I ask the Lord for His peace of mind and heart, to be assured that He will give me the words He wants said and a heart that feels the pain in someone's life.

I still remember and feel the panic in crying out for God's help one December night a few years ago. A neighbor, friend and active church member had died suddenly and unexpectedly. She lived just over a mile away, and I needed and wanted the presence of the Lord quickly to guide me. I knew her husband, children, extended family and friends present would need a comforting presence from me. I said a quick prayer on the way. It is what I call "prayers on the path."

Let's consider some of the events in the lives of God's people where there must have been prayers from the path on the way to meet someone's need.

## The Lord Jesus

Consider some of these emergency calls to Jesus on His path. I know that Jesus could have known what was coming in advance and seemed to be always prepared. In Luke 8.1-42 Jesus is on the way to the home of Jairus, a synagogue leader, to help his only daughter. While Jesus had a destination and opportunity, there came an interruption from a woman afflicted with a hemorrhage that had been going on for 12 years (vs. 43-48). While Jesus was in a hurry to get to the home of Jairus, he was not deterred from meeting an unexpected call for help.

58

While Jesus did later raise Jairus' daughter from the dead (vs. 49-56), she died while Jesus healed the woman with an issue of blood. Unlike the priest and Levite in the story of the Good Samaritan, Jesus was not above being "interrupted" unexpectedly to meet a need in the life of this poor oppressed woman.

In John 11 we read about a real 911 call to Jesus from His good friends Mary and Martha concerning their brother Lazarus. This family is the one family we read about who regularly hosted Jesus and His disciples. This seemed to be a real home to Jesus on several occasions. Even Jesus' own family is not mentioned or spoken of in similar terms in the gospels. What is the response we see from Jesus?

As we know from the record, Jesus waited two days before leaving. Martha and Mary were upset and confused by Jesus' seeming lack of concern and cold-heartedness. It seemed out of character and mysterious for such a close friend as Jesus. I don't think I could get away with this response in the local ministry! What was Jesus thinking? How did He pray for them during the long four-day delay from ministry and care for Lazarus and the family?

No one wants to let people down. I feel certain that Jesus would have been praying for Mary and Martha and the sadness and confusion filling their hearts. Was Jesus praying for their faith, that it would not fail them? Or was he praying for that day when He would arrive and meet them that they would receive Him and understand the lesson He was teaching them? I think Jesus would have been praying all the way on the path to their home. Jesus was about to answer their prayers in a wonderful demonstration of power over death when He delivered Lazarus from the tomb. He must have looked ahead to His own tomb, and the ultimate and final victory over the enemy of death that would be realized on His resurrection day, which would provide the promise of resurrection for all the world.

## The Apostles

In the ministry of Peter in Acts there were many events that most likely challenged him to leave his comfort zone; I will consider two of these. In Acts 9, Peter came to Lydda and healed a man who had been bedridden for eight years. People in the area were aware of this miracle and many turned to Jesus. In that region was the city of Joppa, where there were believers. When a woman in the congregation, a beloved hard worker who had helped many people, unexpectedly died, they remembered that Peter was just twelve miles away at Lydda. They sent men to him in a hurry to urge Peter to come to Joppa.

Question: What was Peter thinking and praying during that twelve-mile journey? What do we think and pray when we are called to an emergency situation at the death of a loved one? I remember being called in the middle of the night when a daughter, wife, mother and grandmother had been taken to the emergency room and was receiving C.P.R. What do you pray and what can you do or say?

By God's grace, Peter raised Dorcas from the dead; God has not given me the power to raise the dead! A minister often finds himself crying out in his heart and mind to the Lord, praying for God's intervention, comfort and healing for the family.

Another event in Peter's ministry is recorded in Acts 10-11. This seemingly impossible situation involved the call of God to go to the house of Cornelius and proclaim the gospel of salvation to the first Gentiles. I have often wondered what Peter was thinking and praying on that journey. This was new, unbroken ground for the church. What would be the outcome and reaction to this mission?

In a wonderful reception and response, Cornelius and his household came to faith and were baptized into Jesus Christ. Peter knew that what they had done was unlawful in the Jewish culture and would even be looked down upon by the church, which was all Jewish at this time.

God prepared Peter through a vision to bring the Gospel to the Gentiles, a new reality for the church. Peter understood that God was doing a "new thing" in the kingdom. In Acts 11 Peter defended his actions and acceptance of this Gentile into fellowship and, to Peter's credit he took six witnesses with him to Caesarea. The church at Jerusalem was persuaded that God sanctioned Cornelius' conversion; they celebrated this revolutionary expansion and outreach of the Gospel.

One evening I received a call from a lady who is in our church. She had fed a stranger who was on her porch; he needed a place to stay for the night. She seemed uncertain and a bit troubled with the whole situation, so I went to her home. There I found a person who told a story of being from another state and having just been released from prison. I was even more surprised that this person had on a dress and lipstick but also sported a five o'clock shadow and had not shaved his legs!

So I prayed along the way and drove them to the local motel, where arrangements had been made for keeping transients for a night. To say the least, I was a bit uncomfortable going into the office to get a room for this person. Afterward, I also informed the police, and they assisted by transporting him to the county line the next morning.

## Paul's Prayers on the Path

In the life and ministry of Paul, his journey often did not take a straight line but rather called for much prayer, patience and wisdom to allow God to lead. Paul spent years of his life in prison, which may have felt like years on the shelf; however, during this period he fulfilled God's plan through writing several letters, many of which are our New Testament books.

In Acts 16.6-8, Paul is preaching and teaching in many places when he comes to a "dead end," not knowing where to go next. The Bible tells us that the Holy Spirit was forbidding him to speak in Asia. Do you ever feel frustrated and locked in, uncertain about what path God has for you? Paul's plan was to wait and pray until God gave him clear direction, which God did. We can think of these times as a "holy pause" in our life, as God prepares us and develops our patience for the next chapter. In God's agenda, some of Paul's greatest work lay ahead.

Another case involved Paul's desire to get back to Thessalonica to encourage and support the believers there (I Thessalonians 2.18). Paul had only been in this city for three Sabbaths before a riot broke out and he had to leave (Acts 17.1-9). These brethren would be infants in their faith and it would be normal that Paul felt an obligation to disciple them further. In

I Thessalonians 2.17-20, we learn of Paul's desire and Satan's opposition to this plan. We sometimes miss or forget the fact that our plans can have Satanic opposition. Paul paints a very dramatic and clear picture of this struggle we must face through prayer and trusting in God. (see Ephesians 6.10-12).

This struggle did not end with the apostles, but goes on in the lives of God's people every day. We fight and win this conflict with God's armor (Ephesians 6.13-17). Paul experienced this same battle and many detours in regard to his desire and plan to get to Rome (Romans 1.13; 15.22-25). It would only be through events in Jerusalem and his arrest that he would finally, after many years, get to Rome.

### The Prophets

The Old Testament prophets faced the same kinds of challenges and were certainly called to be in prayer on the path to deliver God's message in the face of danger and misunderstanding. The prophet Nathan was charged by God to deliver a confrontational parable to King David in II Samuel 12.1-4. David understood the story in this message, but did not anticipate the identity of the-culprit in the parable -- who was David himself! What did Nathan feel while on the path to deliver this message from God to the king?

David was extremely popular. He had the power of life and death over those who would attack him. But David was also "a man after God's own heart," and rather than reject this lesson, he was convicted by it. I would imagine that Nathan prayed with every step he took toward the palace, asking that the Lord would grant him the right attitude to approach the king and the right words to speak.

Like most of us, he would not relish or enjoy this kind of assignment. We prefer to give good news, rather than to rebuke. We do not like to experience rejection when we are trying to be a faithful messenger of God. It would seem to me that Nathan would also be concerned for his future. What if the king responded in anger and disobedience to God? What could happen to King David and his relationship with God because of possible reactions to this message? Most all of us in ministry have seen people react poorly and rebel against God rather than learning and humbling themselves before Him. This is both sad and tragic!

A bizarre story in this vein is found in II Kings 13. God sent a prophet from Judah to King Jeroboam to announce God's coming judgement on Israel (the northern tribes). This unnamed prophet completed his mission successfully, but there was a condition given by the Lord that the prophet was not to eat, drink or stay in that area. This instruction may not have seemed to be central or very important to the assignment, but God cares about the details of obedience. This restriction would prove to be important to God and tragic to the prophet. As he was returning to Judah, a "false" prophet asked him to stay with him. This false prophet claimed to have had a different word from the Lord (vs. 18).

As we pray on the path we must remain focused on God's instructions and message in every detail. This is one reason why contemplative prayer is such a vital aspect of ministry. There have always been and always will be people who claim God has spoken to them, changing the message or the assignment of the messenger. God's judgment came in a most violent and unexpected event in verse 26.

Be warned that Satan lurks in many places and behind many voices. In our prayers on the path we need to always be discerning about the voices and counsel we receive, whether sought after or not. I think the example of the Apostle Paul, on his way to Jerusalem for the last time, provides an illustration for us. Paul had an understanding of what lay ahead, as seen in Acts 20.22-24. He also had warning from the disciples at Tyre in Acts 21.4-6. Then at Caesarea the prophet Agabus and others urged him to not go to Jerusalem (Acts 21.10-12). Paul, because of his prayers and leading from the Holy Spirit, proceeded and left all this in God's hands (Acts 21.13-14). Paul's insight and wisdom came from the retreat of his soul in prayer.

Another person on the path who seemed to not be listening very well was Jonah. Jonah was given a very specific mission to carry out for the Lord: go to Nineveh and cry out against it! But rather than praying on the path, Jonah ran from God and encountered a severe wake-up call (Jonah 1.4-2:10). When this prophet was finally convinced that he ought to obey God and allow God to use him, he went to Nineveh and had tremendous success. The whole city turned from its sin and to God!

Jonah became angry and depressed that God had saved the city. When you think about this, it is shocking. But have you ever known or seen someone so evil that you really did not have a heart to save their soul? Sometimes we just want God to judge them and destroy them!

Consider Jesus' parable of the two sons in Luke 15.11-32. We so often focus on the prodigal that we easily miss the real lesson of the older son who was more lost than the prodigal. That is a picture of the Jewish leaders in Jesus' day who so hated the "sinful" people of their day, and the Gentiles, that they would not allow them into the kingdom. Both Peter and Paul dealt with this problem in the early church. If we are praying and on God's path, then we will not withhold God's grace from any person who is willing to repent and accept Him.

## The Holy Spirit

Another "prayer on the path" comes from Luke 12. God's servants never know what will be encountered along the path. We do not know what we will be called upon to do or say. But, this we can know: God is with us and will supply our need in the moment. In Luke 12 Jesus is teaching about the reaction of some to the gospel and the persecution that will come from others because some people do not want to hear the message of God concerning their sins and destiny.

One of the greatest fears of Christians when it comes to witnessing and sharing our testimony about Jesus is, "What should I say?" We fear the unknown and our own inadequacy in defending our faith and ourselves. Even if we spend time in contemplation we still can feel inadequate and unprepared. Jesus gives words of comfort and encouragement in Luke 12:11-12.

*When they bring you before the synagogues and the rulers and the authorities, do not worry about how or what you are to speak in your defense, or what you are to say; for the Holy Spirit will teach you in that very hour what you ought to say.*

This does not mean we ought not to pray or think before we get to court, but it does mean God will be with us and His Holy Spirit will guide us when we are on His path and praying for His words to fill our mouths.

## Summary

As we have those quiet times and opportunities for contemplation, let us allow them to fill the reservoir of our souls, so that we will have resources to draw upon in our times of urgent need. Jesus often went away to spend the night in prayer. Often this was before a major decision like choosing the twelve apostles. He was also in the Garden of Gethsemane just a few hours before the shame, horror and injustice of the cross. We should take advantage of opportunities to fill our spiritual reservoir which will increase our confidence and assurance of God's presence and help in time of need.

You have a path set before you; it is God's path! As you daily walk in the path as His servant, make prayer your habit and attitude along the way. He will guide you in His will–and make you adequate as you speak His message. He delights in using humble pots of clay in which He has deposited His treasure of life and eternity for the world. Draw deeply on His deposit in you as you journey along!

✠

*After this manner therefore pray:*

*Our Father who is in heaven, Hallowed be your name.*

*Your kingdom come. Your will be done on earth, as it is in heaven.*

*Give us this day our daily bread.*

*And forgive us our debts, as we forgive our debtors.*

*And lead us not into temptation but deliver us from evil: For yours is the kingdom, and the power, and the glory, forever. Amen.*

*Matthew 6:9-13 (KJBT)*

# Prayer & Healing

✠

*Chapter 8*

Ben Murphy

'Once upon a time' a certain group of ministers who call themselves 'The Bardstown Brothers' dedicated themselves to author a book on the topic of *Contemplative Prayer.* I happen to be a member of this venerable group. My thoughts turned immediately to the subject of divine healing, and the correlation between divine healing and contemplative prayer.

Let me say at the outset that I am a firm believer in divine healing. Being raised in the church by Christian parents, I have seen evidence of divine healing throughout my life. But before attempting to link divine healing with the lifestyle of contemplative prayer I should like to (a) begin with a simple definition of divine healing and (b) recount a definition on contemplative prayer.

"Divine healing" is a term used when the miraculous and supernatural activity of God is manifested as it relates to the sick or afflicted among us. It is usually -- but not confined to -- the result of an answer to prayer, whereby a person who is sick or afflicted is made well by the direct intervention of God. Secondly, let me restate that *contemplative prayer* is defined as a practical expression of Paul's exhortation to "pray without ceasing." It is a lifestyle of conscious living in the presence of God and walking in communion with him in everyday life. I will add an even more simplified definition through an illustration.

A good friend of mine, who is a pastor in the Nashville, Tennessee, area once used the term "pistol prayer" for continuous prayer. As we go through our day and various thoughts come to mind we just simply aim our prayer pistol upward and "fire off" an instantaneous prayer to God and move on with our day, but not leaving the need for the prayer out of our conscious thinking. By doing so we naturally are leaving the results by faith to Him who hears and answers prayer. A pistol prayer is a spontaneous form of the contemplative life. It flows from the awareness of His presence in the time of need, as illustrated by numerous examples in our previous chapter.

There is ample evidence of divine healing in Scripture. The healing of the sick is so much a part of the Gospel that no person could possibly preach or teach the entirety of the teachings of Jesus without touching upon the subject of healing. Healing was an integral aspect of the ministry of Jesus. Later it would become one of the mainstays of the doctrinal stamp of the apostles.

Here is one of the many examples of healing in the New Testament. In Acts 14. 8-18 there was a certain event in the city of Lystra where a man crippled from birth heard the preaching of Paul. Verse 9 says that Paul *observed him intently.* (NKJV). The King James Version states that Paul *beheld him and perceived him to be a man of faith.* I have to pause here and picture this or draw a mental image of this in my mind. What was it that went through Paul's thinking process? The fact of the matter is -- and I believe it has to be obvious when we consider the prayer life of Paul -- that Paul gave much thought and even contemplation to the situation. It was intercessory. It was prayer and supplication for the specific need.

Paul perceived! There is no impression in the narrative that Paul just walked by and waved a magic wand, or sprinkled magic pixie dust on the man. Paul's *contemplative* practice was the foundation for his perception into the situation and the prompting of the Holy Spirit. With a loud voice he said to the man, "Stand to thy feet," and the man stood up, leaped around and walked.

In this example we see not only the contemplation that Paul gave to the matter of a needy man, but of action being joined together with prayer. I believe that Paul was a man who, as he walked the countryside from town to town or sailed from port to port, was in continual prayer for the many events that would arise on his missions. There is no doubt that this man was healed of his infirmity by divine intervention.

Some people may debate the role and contemplative aspects of prayer and the inner life as it relates to healing, but there is no debate about scriptural accounts of divine healing. The Scripture is replete with evidence that Jesus and the apostles taught and took part in many such activities.

I believe that the message of Paul in the case in Lystra was based on faith. I also believe there is ample evidence that Paul "prayed without ceasing." Paul was a man of faith and recognized the cripple to be a man of strong faith. Therefore, after contemplative intercession and supplication of the situation, the healing took place. This scripture and many, many others cause me to pause and ask, "Why is this kind of preaching and teaching not taking place more today?" Why does the church leave the sick and infirmed to happenstance, when we have such a marvelous tool as prayer? Why are we not implementing the powerful gift that we have available that we call *contemplative* prayer?

Certainly, if ever it were needed at all, it is needed in the present day in which we live. Paul admonished young Timothy and also us to *"preach the word."* One cannot preach the entirety of the word without preaching divine healing. Again, I believe it to be an integral part of the gospel of Jesus. I will arrive shortly at my point of how contemplative prayer and divine healing intertwine. However, first let me touch on what I believe to be one of the problems that we face today with the subject of teaching and preaching divine healing.

Almost every person in America has television. For years we have been inundated in our homes with the televangelist who purports to miraculous healings, with an "If" attached to it. (Notice I purposely spelled 'If' with a capital letter!) For example, "IF you just send (x-amount of) dollars, we will send this handkerchief to you that has been dipped in oil and baptized in the River Jordan." Promises of divine healing are guaranteed to the faithful, and leave many people disillusioned when the healing does not occur.

If you take notice of the "If," you will notice that the reversal of what is taught in the scriptures is evident, as least as far as Jesus and the healing acts of the apostles is concerned. I have never read in any portion of the gospel where money came first in the scriptural healing process. Divine healing must be sought. It cannot be bought or conjured up.

I believe that Scripture teaches that God in His benevolence expects us to manifest our faith in Him, and not in a trinket for divine healing. Jesus said that anything we ask *in His name* He will do. Asking in the name of Jesus encompasses more than just saying the words. What is implied here is that if we do not ask, we may not receive. That is why Christians are exhorted to pray for one another *that ye may be healed* (James 5.16). Those who are sick are commanded to *call for the elders of the church* to pray with them and for them, and ask God to heal them (James 5.14-15).

In addition, the book of Hebrews tells us that Christians are to *come boldly before the throne of grace that we may obtain mercy and find grace to help in time of need.* All of these instructions are given so that divine healing may be manifested. God is glorified and mankind can rejoice in His goodness.

It should be noted before I continue that there are elements of dissention in the various Christian communities concerning contemplative prayer. Many perceive the contemplative lifestyle and prayer life as solely associated with a monastic style or *centering* type of prayer. Some believe that in order to be fully engrossed in a contemplative lifestyle, one must commit much of his life to meditation and contemplation in silence, with a certain expression lent to even the posture of the body while being in contemplation.

It is easy to become sidetracked with the forms of prayer and thoughts about how contemplative prayer should or should not be approached, while all the time being distracted from praying. So, in the vernacular of the layman, I don't have a dog in that fight. We need to pray because we are motivated by a deep sincerity. We need to pray earnestly.

Remember our working definition is that contemplative prayer is "prayer without ceasing." This is aimed directly at the Christian who is not afforded the time to spend hour upon hour in "silent" contemplation and meditation. It is for the butcher, baker and candlestick maker, who labor through their day and remain in constant accord with the Father, ceaselessly praying through whatever the day holds.

Word comes via text message that Mary has been diagnosed with inoperable cancer and the thought immediately goes to firing up a prayer for Mary. This prayer ascends to the throne, not only at the moment, but at any moment through the day that the thought of Mary comes to mind. That is my idea of a contemplative prayer lifestyle as it is associated with divine healing. It is the inner awareness of Christ's presence in the daily activity of life and need. When we as Christians are made aware of an illness, be it the runny nose of an infant or the most difficult terminal diagnosis of an adult, we should be in "contemplation" of the healing of the one afflicted, even to the point of praying and acting immediately.

A dear lady in a church where I previously served was taken to surgery to remove a small lump from her throat. The surgeon assured her that it was nonmalignant, but for comfort, he would remove it. All too quickly the doctor returned and I knew that something was amiss. He met with the family and told them that she had inoperable throat cancer. Immediately our church and many friends and neighbors, including the doctor, began praying for her. I received a phone call from this lady about two weeks after the diagnosis. She asked me to call the elders of the church and come to her home, anoint her, and pray for her.

Our church did not have designated "elders," but I gathered six of our senior saints and went to her home. We gathered around and anointed her, and I began to pray. In just a few seconds I sensed in my spirit the Lord saying that any further prayer was only words; the job had been done. So I abruptly stopped and informed the group what I believed had happened. Two weeks later, her doctor declared her cancer free, and she lived many more years. It was not the tremendous prayer that I prayed for her that healed her; it was the ongoing, contemplative intercessory prayers of God's people that had reached God and healed her.

I'm sure there are those who say that they prayed unceasingly for healing to come to themselves or a friend or loved one but the healing did not come. What do we say to those people? I don't know if anyone truly has the answer to that question. But I do know for certain that in Mark 11.24, Jesus said, *"Therefore I say unto you, what things soever ye desire when ye pray, believe that ye receive them, and ye shall have them" (KJV)*. This says to me that there must be complete confidence that healing will take place. Faith and doubt don't mix in the same bowl. If we throw up a prayer and then proclaim, "Gee, I hope it works," we are in trouble at the outset. To the disheartened I would merely say this word that Jesus used: BELIEVE. Belief is the key to healing as it relates to contemplative prayer.

Again, notice that Paul did not wait to confer with the elders of the church, or wait for the official verification from the doctors regarding the lame man. He had been in contemplation as he approached Lystra, I'm sure, and immediately joined his prayers with action. It is much like what a friend of mine taught me many years ago when I first entered the pastoral ministry. He said that when he receives a call on the phone of someone in need, he always prays with the person before he ends the conversation on the phone. Then he writes down the request and remains in prayer for that need throughout the days ahead. From that I learned that contemplative prayer or "praying without ceasing" for such needs is an ongoing process.

In the church where I presently serve, we have in our pews bright pink prayer cards on which people list their prayer concerns, then place them in the offering plate when the weekly offering is received. At a later point in the service I will offer a prayer for each person listed. But I do not discard those bright pink cards after the service. They are placed in a prominent place on my desk where I can see them collectively every day. I do not go through and pray individually for these needs daily, but when my eye comes across them I say a prayer; I fire off a pistol shot upward for them. This may not be some people's idea of a contemplative prayer life, but I see it as being as close to Paul's admonition as I can make it.

In conclusion, you may define your prayer life in several ways. You may invest hours in a contemplative prayer routine over a need. That's okay. You may just simply say that you offered an intercessory prayer. That too is admissible in the subject of prayer. You may even be one who takes oil and purposely visits the sick person in need. Whatever your course of action, the bottom line is "pray!" Leave the healing to God, but continue to pray, regardless of the severity of the need.

God wants to see his children at work supporting and showing concern for one another. If time is available, do as Paul did and "contemplate the situation," surely. But when the need arises, no matter where you might be at the moment, "fire off" a prayer -- a "pistol prayer"-- and then keep that need on your heart throughout your day and even the days ahead. Again, I've used the term "I believe" many times in this chapter. But I do believe that the faithful need to continually add to our daily prayer lives. God uses people of prayerful action, not subtraction. So add prayer, and trust God for exponential results!

✠

*And after that they had mocked him, they took the robe off from him, and put his own clothing on him, and led him away to crucify him.*

*And as they came out, they found a man of Cyrene, Simon by name: they compelled him to bear his cross.*

*And when they had come unto a place called Golgotha, that is to say, a place of a skull,*

*They gave him vinegar to drink mingled with gall: and when he had tasted it, he would not drink.*

*And they crucified him, and parted his garments, casting lots: that it might be fulfilled which was spoken by the prophet, They parted my garments among them, and for my clothing they cast lots.*

*And sitting down they watched him there;*

*Matthew 27:31-36 (KJBT)*

# Break the Silence

✠

*Chapter 9*

Cliff Bowman

As I enter the long walkway to the Catholic monastery, there are signs that say, "Silence spoken here!" In amazement, I remember how quiet it was walking to the church for the evening compline service. I was amazed how much I could hear in the "silent zone."

You see, I am a Pentecostal pastor. I am first a follower of Christ, and I am also affiliated with the Church of God, Cleveland, Tennessee. Our churches are known for services that are loud and lively. Sounds of saints shouting praises to God are not uncommon in our worship experience. The sight of passionate people raising their hands in the air and exuberantly singing is very ordinary in the church where I have spent most of my life. I must admit, I like it that way. I enjoy exuberant, energetic worship.

I love the spontaneous expressive environment and someone testifying about what the Lord has done in his or her life, breaking forth in joyful praise. In casual observation one could assume that in a Pentecostal church worship is solely driven by emotion. But that assumption is wrong. For many Pentecostal believers these feelings are anchored in a deeply rooted faith in Jesus, and the assurance He gives of our salvation and future. So our congregation is encouraged to push through the temptation to keep it to yourself, encouraged to "break the silence" and praise the Lord, to give testimony for who He is and the great things He has done.

There is order in the Pentecostal service, even though it is rarely written down: a Bible-based sermon, prayer and singing. Our church is not foolish about Christian worship; we embrace the ultimate authority of Scripture that guides our worship, and we judge all spiritual manifestations by the Scripture. So, as in the personal Christian experience, there are corporate times of subdued silence and lively loudness. I find this mixture to correlate with the ebb and flow of the Christian life. You never know exactly what will happen.

## Silence Speaks Loudly

As a member of a Pentecostal church I sometimes think that the louder we are, the more spiritual we are. Certainly loud worship can have its place. "Shout unto the Lord with the voice of triumph" has biblical precedence. But silence is an equally valid spiritual expression as well. Psalms 46.10 admonishes us to "be still and know that I am God." I have personally learned that silence is a megaphone that conveys over the noise of this world. Turning to Christ in the silence refreshes my soul. My times of deliberate silence add depth and value to the louder moments of my vocal praise of God.

Having said all that, I want to make an observation about silence. It came to me while visiting a Catholic monastery. Throughout the day, the monks pray, sing Psalms and practice silence. The silence of the monks and the chapel full of quiet worshipers spoke loudly to me. We sang together the Psalms. The message was loud and clear. It was God's Word reflected back to Him in an evening prayer. That was all that was spoken. The silent reflection leads us away from the noise, and in a retreat of the soul to the roots of life in Christ.

## Reflection
*Who Do We Reflect and How?*

There is a mountain in Virginia between Waynesboro and Charlottesville called Afton Mountain. It is notorious for heavy fog. There are signs as you begin the ascent warning the driver of this possibility. I have driven up this mountain when the fog was so thick the road in front of you could not be seen. What saved me were the reflectors in the middle of the road and the lights positioned on the edge of the road.

According to the transportation department these sidelights can be turned on when heavy fog is detected. Anyone who has driven this road is aware that it is next to impossible to navigate without the reflectors and the lights. The small reflector in the middle of the road reflects my vehicle's lights. It is reflecting the light from my headlights back to me. The lights on the side of the road are powered by another source, giving the driver extra warning of the treacherous edges.

The follower of Christ is very much like those reflector lights. The light we shine is a reflection of Jesus. The light we show is the power of God at work within us. The level of brightness depends on our position and

81

connection to Him. In the Bible we read about a man who spent forty days and nights on a mountain praying and fasting. When Moses came off that mountain the people noticed that his face was shining. He was unaware of this. The people were so afraid of Moses that he had to cover his face when he was in their presence.

The word for "shine" in the text referring to Moses means "to protrude." It was more than a halo effect. It was more than glow. It was light protruding from his face. The apostle Paul told the Philippians that they were "to shine as lights in a crooked and perverse world" (Philippians 2.15). The word for "light" here is radiance. The same word is used to describe the holy city New Jerusalem as it comes down from Heaven.

How do we reflect the light of Jesus? I believe it comes from spending time in the presence of Jesus, reflecting upon Him and His word. For the reflector in the middle of the road to properly reflect, it has to be in the path of oncoming light. For lights that are power-driven to work, they must be connected to a power source. To reflect Jesus I must be in a place where I can intercept His light and be intimately connected to Him. The best place for such intimate fellowship with Christ is in prayer.

Jesus reminds us that private prayer precedes any powerful public ministry. In my private moments of prayer, I am inwardly reflecting upon God, Scripture and my life in Christ. Then when I enter the public sphere I have light to reflect and shine forth. It is not my own light. It is not my own ideas or opinions. It is not even my own story. It is Christ's light, both reflecting and emanating from me. Jesus did say, "You are the light of the world."

Similarly, Paul talks about "prayer without ceasing." This is the proper spiritual position to reflect the most light. But how can we pray without ceasing? Paul did not mean that each person must pray twenty-four hours a day without ever stopping. Common sense informs that this is impossible.

Perhaps the best way to understand "prayer without ceasing" is to use an analogy to distinguish between the words "continual" and "continuous." Continuous prayer is like the water faucet when wide open. The blasting water can cause flooding, until the faucet is shut off. Continual prayer is like a dripping faucet. A drip is not continuous flow of water. There are intervals when there is no drip; then a drip lingers and slips out of the faucet. It is *continual*, but it is not *continuous*. I believe it is possible to be in a continual state of prayer, but not be continuously praying.

While I do have my set times of prayer, I realize that I'm praying at intervals throughout the day. I am praying for the reader, as I'm writing this chapter. I am practicing what Paul admonished -- "pray without ceasing" – which I see as an evangelical definition of contemplative prayer. It is an attitude of prayer that positions me to best reflect Jesus to those around me. It is the continual praying that connects me to the power source -- shining as a light in this crooked and perverse world.

Reflecting the light of Jesus in the course of a day is the result of being in fellowship with Christ in personal, prayerful devotion. Light reflects out and penetrates the darkness, dispelling its power. May God bless you as you reflect upon Jesus and as you reflect Him to those in darkness.

I am thankful for those reflectors and lights on Afton Mountain, and those who strategically placed them. On at least two occasions I would have been forced to stop my vehicle in the foggy darkness if they were not in place. There are sinners trying to find their way in the darkness, and to them you reflect His light. They do not know how to find their way in the darkness. Followers of Christ are the reflectors and the lights. Love God and love people to Christ.

## Conclusion

I have learned to be comfortable with silence, and find it helpful in my Christian devotion. The silence allows me to reflect upon Christ and my faith in Him. My sins are forgiven! Silence does speak loudly. But the heart connected to Christ in prayer naturally overflows with His joy. Rejoicing in the Lord is the vehicle. The rocks do not need to cry out, when we have been given a voice. Even though silence speaks loudly, silence still needs a voice at times. Sometimes we should break the silence with shouts of joy! Even those in darkness need to hear how Christ has brought us into the light. Because of what Jesus has done, we have the needed permission to break the silence, with a triumphant shout:

"PRAISE THE LORD!"

Try it!

# God's Exclamation Point!

✠

*Chapter 10*

Greg Sergent

Quiet walks prompt deep reflection within me. Strolling leisurely through the garden at the Abbey of Gethsemani, my sight was drawn to the rows of crosses marking the graves of departed monks. Dedicated to their monastic order, vows of silence and prayerful intercession, now all that remains of their devotion are crosses that bear their names. This is where it ends for the monks, and monastic activity. The cross stands firmly planted in the earth, just like an exclamation point at the end of a sentence. It quietly shouts that the work is finished. No words are spoken. No words are needed.

Prayers are offered daily. Since the abbey's inception in 1848, prayers are offered seven times a day by the faithful, interspersed with the work of making fudge. Outside the cloistered walls of prayer and work, the haunting shadow of death widens and lurks as a cold hand to silence even the few words spoken in prayer. All that remains lies in the darkness of the earthen sod. Buried alongside a community of departed brothers, an empty seat and one less chanting voice silences an already quiet place.

For the monk and the Christian pilgrim, the cross makes a definitive statement. It is the sacrifice and death of the self- life. It is a living, daily death, to the greater call of vows, prayers and the Christ-life, and walking in the pilgrim way. It is a marker of a life well-lived.

The pilgrim walks the way to lonely Golgotha with Christ, and co-identifies with the crucified Savior. The pilgrim life is one of a living sacrifice of oneself being set apart for worship and service. Like the monks, our walk among the tombs and gravestones remind us of the brevity of life -- of our own mortality. And in the recesses of our conscious we sense death's quiet presence.

Death sobers us up! Intoxicated by the world's noisy clamor and frantic busyness time slips away. We speed along in a stupor. Then death encroaches and forces us to face the business of eternity. Death confronts us to ponder life's meaning in the search. It is our wake-up call to calibrate life toward meaning. The contemplative discipline enables this process of spiritual formation.

We need an instrument to align with -- a starting point. God gives us one. He suspends the cross as a definitive marker for our time-limited lives. Its beams reach up and widely extend outward. In a strange way, the cross aligns and orders the inner life with meaning and purpose. Like the Apostle Paul's analogy, we submit to rugged cross beams and piercing spikes. We identify with the Crucified One. Like Him I live, yet "not I, but Christ who lives in me" (Galatians 2.20).

## The Cross
*God's Exclamation Point*

There is nothing glamorous about the cross. In reality, it is odd to cherish the emblem as an ornament for adornment. In human history we see that the cross represents failure and is antithetical to any definition of success. Its claim to notoriety is a shameful instrument of execution, reserved for the vilest criminals. Yet God chooses an instrument of shame to secure our greatest hope and freedom. What a paradox!

The empty tomb is evidence of the Savior conquering death so we can fully understand the meaning of the cross. Death's status has changed. Because of the resurrection, death is now only a passing shadow. Light and new life burst forth from Christ's empty tomb. Death's stranglehold is broken, and we have passed from death to life.

We have good news of life, and the greatest source of hope. It means real life change and transformation for the broken and those dead in trespasses and sin, through trusting Christ by faith. Why? Because there is Christ's resurrection life living within the believer. Christ's words resound: "Those who believe in me will never die" (John 11.26). The great writer and theologian Thomas Aquinas declared, "The Cross to me is certain salvation. The Cross is that which I ever adore. The Cross of the Lord is with me. The Cross is my refuge."

The cross reaches up to the heavens from our perspective. The cross draws our gaze upward as it should. However, from heaven's perspective it is incarnated love, being born of a virgin, condescending in a great feat of rescue. Mysteriously, this was God's eternal plan decreed in time, before the foundation of the world. Standing tall as an exclamation point in human history, the cross captures the imagination of believers and skeptics alike. It compels a closer look, and firmly withstands a thorough examination of even the most doubtful.

However, the richness of the cross lies in contemplative wonder. The heavy-laden heart finds rest in the soul at Calvary and the depth of love in the display. Isaac Watts captures the wonder of the cross in the thought-provoking hymn, *When I Survey the Wondrous Cross.*

> *When I survey the wondrous cross,*
> *On which the Prince of Glory died,*
> *My richest gain I count but loss,*
> *And pour contempt on all my pride.*

To those embracing Christ's nail-pierced hand, the cross is the cherished instrument and symbol of salvation. His holy hand reaches out and meets the guilty and the broken hearted with grace, mercy and forgiveness. Christ, our substitute for sin, pays our sin debt and then rends the veil, opening to all the Holy of Holies into the presence of God Himself.

"It is finished," uttered from the cross, meant the completion of God's great rescue and the destruction of death manifested on resurrection morning. Christ, then, is the believer's Righteousness and access for Holy Communion with the Heavenly Father.

## Take Up Your Cross

It is interesting that Jesus equates following Him with taking up a cross. Jesus, I believe, is saying, "If you are my disciple, you better count the cost."

Do you know what it will cost you?

> Personal goals, aspirations or dreams?
> The understanding of family or friends?
> Social status?
> Prestige?

You will be stretched to the limits of your own personal comforts, and may even give your life. The disciples counted the cost and bought into his message. They forsook all and followed Jesus. They laid down their pursuits and business. They listened, learned and obeyed as best they could. In their thinking, Jesus would bring sweeping social change, and they were in on it. But were they really hearing what he was saying?

Following Jesus was great for about three years, and then seemingly the whole enterprise fell apart. They had no clue that following Jesus would lead them to experience the betrayal of a friend, a mock trial, public opinion turning against Jesus, and watching Jesus face cruel-mockery and a beating. And then the instrument of shameful execution was thrust upon his beaten human frame -- the Cross.

Jesus stumbled along the Via Dolorosa, carrying his cross. The disciples knew where this was going -- to a lonely hill outside of town. Crushing down upon Him, under its weight, the dust was ready to devour the Son of Man. His fate was just like every other man's. Death was impending and certain. His disciples winced and turned away. In every sense of the word, Golgotha was a forsaken hill. He was forsaken by those who had once claimed to be His closest friends.

Indeed, the darkest hour of the cross remained. A forsaken hour, with words uttered from a despairing soul. "My God, My God, why have you forsaken me?" was his gasping cry, and then the sun's light darkened. He was ultimately forsaken! He was completely rejected! His final rejection opens a door for you and me. With a loving embrace our acceptance before the Father is secured. In reality, then, the cross He carried was my cross, bearing my shame and my sin. What a paradox! I am ultimately accepted through his ultimate rejection!

That is something to seriously reflect upon; yes, even contemplate. Wonder in! We do that in our commemorative meal. We count the cost he paid for us, smitten with awe of Christ's matchless love displayed on the Cross! Such love draws us, compels us and demands nothing less than our life totally surrendered to Christ. Counting the cost in self-examination, the pilgrim leaves all selfish ambition and follows Christ. It is the denial of the self-life, but in exchange, the gaining of something greater. We gain Christ's resurrection-life and His joyful accompaniment in our journey. Our hearts burn with renewed hope and life, just like the disciples on the road to Emmaus.

I think of countless missionaries who have boarded boats and planes to relocate far from the comforts of home and the support of family and friends, giving their very lives for the message they believe. History is replete with examples of many who faithfully shared the message in the face of danger and death.

I also think of those whose sacrifice is behind the cloistered walls of consecrated intercession for a world filled with sin, suffering, destruction and death. As I understand it, this is the prayerful activity of monastic life. Alone in a quiet place, the intercessor stands between God and man pleading to the Father for the souls of people in the throes of spiritual death, as the missionary stands at the tomb of the spiritually dead, declaring resurrection life and pleading for sinners to repent and embrace God's gift of new life. The ministry of reconciliation on a practical level is the work of prayer and evangelism. Both are equally important in heaven's economy. Pray to the Father, and plead with man! Carry that cross; Jesus did.

Don't worry or fret about your inadequacy or failures. The message of the cross stands firmly in the middle of this world's messes. It stands when the winds of change blow culture off course. It stands in lonely, forsaken and painful places. It brings light to the dark places where shame holds the captive in fear. It penetrates man's deepest existential questions. And in the darkness Jesus meets us -- right there. Jesus -- the innocent, suffering Savior -- lavishes forgiveness and healing, instead of revenge and retribution. God's love pours out upon all at the cross. His gift of love triumphs human hatred in all forms there. It is good news for all generations and all times. So, let whosoever come... receive!

Suspend the cross high on the ash heaps of human heartache and the vilest of sins. It will stand! And those who squarely face it can exchange beauty for ashes. Its power can pierce the soul as the marker of God's faithfulness and claim upon us. "Accepted" is spoken over those who meet Jesus at the cross, where they acknowledge guilt, shame and brokenness. But one must "take up his cross and follow" in sharing and living this life-transforming gospel...living so genuinely and transparently that what is seen is nothing less than the life and love of Christ pouring from us.

So "take up your cross and follow." You have more to gain than to lose. Follow in the light, and follow when the darkness seems to surround you. Follow when it is convenient, and when it is neither convenient nor comfortable. Follow on lofty mountaintops in its breathtaking awe, and follow in the valley. Keep your eyes on Christ--and follow.

> Follow completely!
> Follow sincerely!
> Follow wholly!

As you do, share in word and in deed God's exclamation point in time! It is the emblem of the contemplative life and spiritual vibrancy. It is where God chooses to meet us. The cross stands as a marker on the monk's grave and as an exclamation point to a life finished well. Christian pilgrim, the cross remains as God's exclamation point over you!

> *Forbid it, Lord that I should boast,*
> *Save in the death of Christ my God!*
> *All the vain things that charm me most,*
> *I sacrifice them to His blood.*
> *~Isaac Watts*

# Jesus is Knocking

✟

*Conclusion*

Greg Sergent

I have always found religious art intriguing. A mid-19th century artist, William Hunt, portrays Christ as the light-bearer in his popular painting entitled "The Light of the World." Gazing at this piece of fine art invites deeper speculation and holy imagination. Surrounded by the darkness, Jesus the light-bearer is standing at the door. He is knocking at this door that is seldom used and obviously unkempt.

Vines and overgrowth encroach upon the door's usefulness. Upon closer observation, Jesus is holding a lantern to a door without an outside handle. The door can only be opened from the inside. Knock, knock, knock! He is waiting. Is there anyone inside who hears? Who inside is even aware that someone is at the door?

The meaning is obvious: Jesus is seeking fellowship and personal communion with us. He takes the initiative for our presence. A Lutheran minister, O. Hallesby, of the early 20th century, describes the essence of contemplative prayer as letting Jesus come into our hearts. Much like the meaning of this painting, Hallesby contended that Jesus moves us to pray. Jesus moves in our ineptness and inability and asks as He did of his sleeping disciples, "Will you not tarry with me for one hour?"

Similarly, in the Revelation of John, he describes a church adorned with the grandeur of worldly success, but poor, naked and blind spiritually. Jesus is on the outside of the church bearing His name, but the building is devoid of His presence. He remains on the outside. So, Jesus knocks.

> *Behold, I stand at the door and knock.*
> *If anyone hears My voice and opens the door,*
> *I will come in to him*
> *and dine with him, and he with Me.*
> *(Revelation 3.20)*

I must confess, this verse has always disturbed me. I find it personally troubling to think that Jesus might be standing outside the church where I serve, or outside the core of my life and ministry. You see, I have experienced how my busy life and the cares of good and even religious activity can replace genuine devotion to Christ. The overgrowth of life's busy cares often crowds the entrance of my heart's door. Those weeds seem to really grow quickly.

Deafened by the noisy clamor within, I cannot hear the knock outside my door. Let your imagination run as you speculate about the religious activities, from board room meetings to banquet socials, programs, and schedules going on behind the closed doors of our churches. His presence could bring so much meaning to what has become routine and mundane to the religiously initiated.

Might Jesus be at the door?  Is Jesus knocking?

Am I in a stupor from my slumber, that I do not hear the knock at the door?  Yet, Jesus continues to knock.  Yes, His love compels a patient, continued knocking, a compelling desire for fellowship.

The church today does not lack in ornate structures, state of the art programs, modern technologies, great music and slick marketing.  I must confess, I enjoy all these amenities of church life today.  But there is an inherent danger of becoming comfortable with material symbols of a successful ministry.  The early church had none of these, yet had tremendous success as the larger community observed a Spirit-empowered body of believers.

Prayer was the program and organization of the early church and, consequently, its success.  They "prayed without ceasing," fervently imploring Heaven's throne-room that "God's will be done on earth as in heaven."  As a result, the world noted that *they had been with Jesus*.  The early church turned their world upside down.

What happens when the door of the heart is opened and heeds Jesus' knocking?  We enjoy the fullness of Jesus' presence with us.  This is communion with the Master at His finest.  We benefit from the full nourishment of the soul -- the very life of God.

This is an all-out soul retreat to the sanctuary of God.  So in our greatest weakness and infirmity, we get the richness of the Godhead in our spiritual home.  A soul retreat offers the greatest potential for fulfillment of the apparent needs and not-so-apparent needs of our life. It is the Christ-life, at work and operational in our deepest needs through His presence.

Dear friend, hear the knock at the door. Be stilled from the frantic busyness. Open the door of sweet communion and fellowship. The soul was made for such a retreat. It needs such a safe place for rest. Jesus is patiently waiting, and even longing for time together where a taste of eternity exists.

Open the door! Fall into the sweet embrace of the heavenly Father. He ushers the weary and worn soul into a joyous retreat. Find the bread of life and cup of blessing. It satisfies spiritual hunger. A thirsty soul is quenched with the refreshing water of life.

Jesus is knocking. Open the Door!

# Discussion Questions

The Bardstown Brothers prayerfully hope that this body of work is beneficial in your spiritual formation and prayer life. For the serious student of prayer, a study guide with questions is presented for your consideration and/or for facilitating small group discussion.

### Contemplative Prayer
*Chapter One*

1.  Have Paul's words "pray without ceasing" in I Thessalonians 5.17 caused you guilt?

2. What has been your interpretation of "pray without ceasing"?

3. Discuss Jeff's statement: "In reality the life of prayer has nothing to do with posture or words or place. It is all about a relationship with Jesus."

4. How did this essay help you in your prayer life?

### "Silence Spoken Here"
*Chapter Two*

1.  What comes to mind when you think of nuns and monks?

2.  Why do you think Jesus often retreated to be alone?

3. Does silence make you uncomfortable? Why? Why not?

4. Discuss Pascal's statement: "All of humanity's problems stem from man's inability to sit quietly in a room alone."

## Come & Dine
### Chapter Three

1. Do you often come home from a vacation more exhausted than when you left? Why? Why not?

2. Name some ways you can take your soul on a "soul retreat."

3. Discuss what Communion means to you personally, and what it means to the Church as a whole.

4. What is your understanding of how fellowship is expressed and experienced in the Lord's Supper?

5. Discuss Greg's statement: "We experience the sacred in the common activity of breaking bread and sharing drink."

## Ritual & Liturgy
### Chapter Four

1. Are you comfortable with the words "ritual" and "liturgy"? Why? Why not?

2. Do you agree with Garrett's statement: "Christian ritual, in the proper sense, is to draw the believer into a

deeper relationship with God, to hear and abide in His presence"? If so, how?

3. Name something you do in your walk with Christ that can be called a ritual.

4. Do all churches have a "liturgy"?

5. Discuss how a prayer routine might help establish spiritual roots.

## Biblical Meditation
### Chapter Five

1. Does "Christian" come to mind when you hear the words "meditation" and "contemplation"? If not, what does?

2. What is the difference between *meditation* and *contemplation*?

3. How would you define/describe biblical meditation?

4. How do you think biblical meditation can help you in your spiritual growth?

5. Discuss the correlation between the Word of God and the will of God. Why is praying the Word of God important?

## Nature's Sanctuary
### Chapter Six

1. Has God ever used His creation to remind you of something necessary for your walk of faith?

2.   What does Mitch mean by the words, "That doesn't change the fact that I'm here"?

3.   How is creation God's witness to the world?

4.   Take a prayer walk in the outdoors and note your awareness of the Creator in your prayer experience.

## Prayers from the Path
### *Chapter Seven*

1.   Discuss Carl's presentation of "contemplative prayer."

2.   Which example in Carl's essay helped you the most?

3.   Carl speaks on a "daily attitude of prayer." What do you think he means?

## Prayer & Healing
### *Chapter Eight*

1.   Discuss Ben's statement: "Divine healing must be sought; it cannot be bought or conjured up."

2.   How has this essay encouraged you in praying for the sick?

3.   But what if God chooses not to heal?

4.   Discuss the various aspects of healing and wholeness.

## Break the Silence
*Chapter Nine*

1. Discuss Cliff's statement: "To reflect Jesus I must be in a place to intercept His light and intimately connect to Him. The best place for such intimate fellowship with Christ is in prayer."

2. Discuss the difference between "continuous prayer" and "continual prayer."

3. Do you agree with Cliff's statement, "I believe it is possible to be in a continual state of prayer, but not be continuously praying"?

4. In what way is the Holy Spirit encouraging you to "break the silence" and reflect the light?

## God's Exclamation Point
*Chapter Ten*

1. Discuss Greg's statement: "The cross stands firmly planted in the earth, just like an exclamation point at the end of a sentence."

2. Discuss the paradox: God chooses an instrument of shame to secure our greatest hope and freedom.

3. What are some worldly affections that challenge the believer's affection to Christ and carrying our cross?

4. Discuss the role of the cross in your prayer life, spiritual formation and ministry.

✠

*Give ear to my words, O Lord,
consider my meditation.*

*Hearken unto the voice of my cry, my
King, and my God: for unto you I will
pray.*

*My voice you shall hear in the
morning, O Lord; in the morning will
I direct my prayer unto you, and will
look up.*

*Psalm 5:1-3 (KJBT)*

Dr. Jerry Mattingly is no stranger to the "Retreat of the Soul." He has led others on the contemplative journey for many years. The Louisville, Kentucky, native is the founder of the Bardstown Retreat. He has participated in planned sabbaticals in many academic communities. He serves the Lord as an ordained minister of Christian Churches, training students at Johnson University in Knoxville, Tennessee, as professor of Intercultural Studies and directing the Honors Program.

As an Old Testament research scholar, he has published works in both history and archaeology. Through his research endeavors he has made 53 trips to 16 countries in the United Kingdom, Europe and Middle East. He has 16 archaeological field sessions in Jordan, Israel and Greece and has served as the co-director of Karak Resources Project in Central Jordan from 1995-2014.

He holds a Ph.D. from the Southern Baptist Theological Seminary in Louisville, Kentucky, and M.Div. and B.A. from Cincinnati Christian University in Cincinnati, Ohio. He enjoys classic movies, reading, traveling and museums. He and his wife Pam have two adult children.

This collection of reflections on the contemplative life is written in his honor.

 Dick McGuirk, lovingly referred to as "Skip," is the heart and soul of the Bardstown Retreat. He is an original Bardstown Brother. For many years he served as the Retreat organizer, but he is no longer able to participate due to his declining health. His spirit and presence are still very much a part of our annual retreat.

Dick's life can be characterized by faith, family and calling. Dick graduated the University of Pittsburgh.

After a job layoff in the 1970s both Dick and Margie answered the Lord's calling into the vocational ministry. They moved to Knoxville, Tennessee, attending Johnson University, pursuing a degree in Preaching and Pastoral ministry. After graduation they moved to Jeffersonville, Indiana, in 1979 and began a pastoral ministry, where he would retire.

Dick lost his precious wife to cancer in the mid-80s (as well as a son, granddaughter, sister and mother, all within a couple of years). Through his losses, he persevered in preaching the Word of God, uniting Christians for fellowship and worship. He has been actively involved and encouraged starting up new congregations in the southern Indiana area. *Retreat of the Soul* expresses the Bardstown Brothers' love and deep appreciation for him and his faithful servant leadership through the years as an example of the contemplative life.

Greg Sergent has been the lead pastor of Glamorgan Chapel in Wise, Virginia over 25 years. He earned a Ph.D. in Theology from Trinity Theological Seminary, a M.A. from Luther Rice Seminary and a B.S. from the University of Virginia's College at Wise. His passion is life-application Bible teaching. *The Christ Life: Discovering your Destiny in Christ through Understanding the Bible* is his most recent book.

Along with pastoral duties, he has served in various capacities among Free Will Baptist associational endeavors. He has also presented numerous training seminars on spiritual care as a hospice chaplain. He is married to Teresa and has two adult children, Andrew & Rachel, and a grandson, Isaac. He enjoys guitar, singing and songwriting, and worship leading. He has been one of the Bardstown Brothers for 6 years, and served as lead editor of the "Retreat of the Soul."

 Jim Wells hails from Romney, West Virginia, but now makes his home in Virginia, where he has served as the pastor of the Norton Christian Church since 1984.

Jim is married to his college sweetheart , Karen Ward. They have three adult children and seven grand-children. He holds a B.A. and M.A. from Johnson University, Knoxville, Tennessee, and has pursued additional studies at Emmanuel Christian Seminary in Johnson City, Tennessee.

He is the recognizable voice of "Bright Spots," airing regionally on radio stations since 1994. He has been a member of the Bardstown Brothers for more than 25 years and serves as the retreat coordinator. Jim is a contributing editor of "Retreat of the Soul".

 Jeff Noel, a native of Pittsburgh, Pennsylvania, is a 1982 graduate of Johnson University in Knoxville, Tennessee, and is a 1986 graduate of The Southern Baptist Theological Seminary in Louisville, Kentucky.

Jeff is married to Linda Stewart Noel who is from Elizabethtown, Kentucky. Jeff and Linda have one child, Marie Layne, who is a student at Auburn University preparing to be a veterinarian.

In January of 2009 he answered the call to serve as the lead pastor at *Grace Heartland Church* in Elizabethtown, Kentucky. Jeff also serves as an adjunct professor in Spiritual Formation and Ministry for the Louisville extension of Johnson University, and presents seminars on Prayer and Spiritual Leadership as the National Coordinator for the *National Prayer Committee*. Jeff is a founding member of the Bardstown Brothers, and coordinates our retreat activities.

Pastor Cliff Bowman is an ordained bishop in the Church of God (Cleveland, Tennessee). He was born in Lynchburg, Virginia and is happily married to Sharon Kay Johnson of Hartsville, Tennessee.

Cliff graduated from Lee University with a B.A. in Biblical Education. He and Sharon have one son, Matthew. He has served the Stevens Church of God in Wise, Virginia, since February 1997. Cliff enjoys anything historical and is an avid Washington Redskins fan. He has been a Bardstown brother for 6 years.

 Mitch Estep grew up in Appalachian Mountains, where "roughing it" was normal and "upcycling" was called "making do." He graduated in 2004 from Johnson University in the Great Smoky Mountains, then youth pastored for a time under the vast expanse of the Midwest sky.

Mitch currently serves a small Eastern Kentucky congregation, Beefhide First Alliance Church. He has been a youth minister, carpenter, camp chaplain, Boy Scout leader, backpacking guide, rock climber, and wild plant and mushroom eater. His most exciting, challenging, and rewarding adventure role is "husband" to Katie and "dad" to their 5 kids. Mitch made his vows to the Bardstown Brotherhood in 2011, and seeks silence in any natural place possible.

Garrett Ward Sheldon is the senior pastor of First Baptist Church in Big Stone Gap, Virginia. He is a professor of Political Theory, Constitutional Law, and Religion & Politics at the University of Virginia's College at Wise.

He grew up in Wisconsin and attended the University of New Mexico earning his B.A. (summa cum laude, 1977) and Rutgers University earning his M.A. and Ph.D. (1983). He has studied or been a visiting scholar at Princeton Theological Seminary; Wycliffe Hall, Oxford; the University of Vienna, Austria; and Trinity College, Dublin, Ireland.

Along with being a Jeffersonian Scholar with numerous academic books to his credit, he is also an author of the popular book "What Would Jesus Do?" He lives on a farm in Powell Valley, Virginia, and is married to Elaine. They have two children: Gwendolyn and Peter. The Rev. Dr. Sheldon has been a Bardstown Brother for 6 years.

 Carl Roudebush was born and reared in Canton, Ohio. He serves as minister of Windfall Christian Church in Windfall, Indiana, and has since 1985. His pastoral ministry has spanned almost 40 years with his first ministry being at the First Christian Church in Etowah, Tennessee (1978-1985).

He holds a Bachelor of Arts from Johnson Bible College in Knoxville, Tennessee, and a Master of Ministry from Kentucky Christian College in Grayson, Kentucky (1984).

He and Marty Roudebush raised three children, and they have five grandchildren and three great grand-children. Carl is an original Bardstown Brother.

Ben Murphy has been in public ministry for over 40 years. With a booming bass voice, he began in public ministry as a music minister, where he served for seventeen years. He has been in pastoral ministry for the past thirty years.

Ben is from West Frankfort, Illinois where he attended West Frankfort public schools, Southeastern Illinois Junior College in Harrisburg, Illinois, and the Gulf Coast Bible College in Houston, Texas.

He has ministered in Illinois, Indiana and Texas in music ministry, and held pastorates in Illinois, Alabama and Virginia with the Church of God, Anderson, Indiana. He has shared forty-seven years of marriage with his wife Diana and together they have a son, daughter and six grandchildren. Ben has been a Bardstown Brother for 6 years.

 Rick Absher has completed 38th year of ministry. He has pastored in Indiana and West Virginia and most recently served a General Baptist congregation which is in Carmi, Illinois.

Rick is a graduate of Johnson University in Knoxville, Tennessee. For the past twenty years he has been involved in the Karak Research Project, which is a multidisciplinary archaeological research team. His travels have been in Central Jordan, where he has explored written accounts of the early travelers on the Karak Plateau within the ancient kingdom of Moab.

Rick is married to Terri, a teacher, and they have a son, Jonathan, who lives and ministers in Knoxville, Tennessee. Rick has attended the Bardstown Retreat since its inception.

Elmer Lester participated in the Bardstown Retreat for several years until his health prevented him from doing so. He served as pastor of First Church of God in Bristol, Tennessee, and is founding Pastor of Christian Fellowship Church, Kingsport, Tennessee.

Elmer formerly served with the Latter Day Saints Church as branch president in East Tennessee. After much study and prayer he left the LDS Church and was ordained into the Christian ministry by Norton Christian Church, Norton, Virginia.

A respected business owner, he operated Auto World and Community Motors in Big Stone Gap, Virginia. Good friends affectionately call him "The Godfather" for making them offers they could not refuse. He is sought out by many souls who seek his gentle wisdom and encouragement. He welcomes anyone who stops by for a visit. Elmer and his wife, Richalene, have three children, four grandchildren and two great grand-children, and countless friends.

CPSIA information can be obtained
at www.ICGtesting.com
Printed in the USA
FFOW02n2326250917
40375FF